Contents

RabbitMQ Introduction 1

RabbitMQ Setup 3

Installing Erlang 3

    Installing RabbitMQ 5

    Starting RabbitMQ Server 5

    Enabling web management plugin 7

    Web Management plugin 8

RabbitMQ Exchanges 9

What are the Exchanges? 9

    Direct Exchange 9

    Adding Exchanges 13

RabbitMQ Queues 14

    Adding queue 20

Binding in RabbitMQ 23

RabbitMQ Users 24

    Creating Users 26

    Setting privilege to access virtual hosts 27

RabbitMQ Virtual Hosts 28

Creating Virtual host 29

    Creating Users 30

    Setting privilege to access virtual hosts 31

Connections 33

Channels 35

Publishing Message 37

Reading Message 39

Delete Message 41

Publish Message Using C# to RabbitMQ 42

Using RabbitMQ Direct Message Exchanges with .Net Application 54

Using RabbitMQ Topic Message Exchanges with .Net Application 63

Using RabbitMQ Fanout Message Exchanges with .Net Application 76

Using RabbitMQ Headers Message Exchanges with .Net Application 87

RabbitMQ Introduction

What is RabbitMQ?

RabbitMQ an AMQP message broker is the most popular open source and cross-platform message broker.

It is built on Erlang which is also used by WhatsApp for messaging.

RabbitMQ is also a way to exchange data between applications such as a message sent from .Net application can be read by a Node.js application or Java application.

RabbitMQ is lightweight and easy to deploy on premises and in the cloud. It supports multiple messaging protocols. RabbitMQ can be deployed in distributed and federated configurations to meet high-scale, high-availability requirements.

Why and when should we Use RabbitMQ?

We should use RabbitMQ because it is open source and easy to use with many languages such as .Net, Java, Python, Ruby, Node Js.

We can use RabbitMQ to remove some heavy work from our web application such as sending Reports in Emails in Excel or Pdf format's or sending email, SMS or another task such as a trigger to some other applications to start processing.

Nowadays most people do all this task into single application sending emails or SMS, reports which bit heavy task which is also handled by IIS if you separate this task then IIS will get more space (memory) to serve more request.

After understanding a bit about RabbitMQ next we are going to Install Erlang and RabbitMQ on Windows.

What is AMQP?

The Advanced Message Queuing Protocol (AMQP) is an open standard application layer protocol for message-oriented the defining features of AMQP are message orientation, queuing, routing (including point-to-point and publish-and-subscribe), reliability and security.

It was developed by JPMorgan and iMatix Corporation.

Key Features

AMQP was designed with the following main characteristics as goals:

- Security
- Reliability
- Interoperability
- Standard
- Open

Various Client Libraries

RabbitMQ support various number of operating systems and various language and it's have various clients for different languages.

1. .Net
2. Java
3. Spring Framework
4. Ruby
5. Python
6. PHP
7. Objective-C and Swift
8. JavaScript
9. GO
10. Perl

RabbitMQ Setup

In this part, we are going to learn how to Setup RabbitMQ in step by step way.

1. What is Erlang
2. Downloading Erlang
3. Installing Erlang
4. Downloading RabbitMQ
5. Installing RabbitMQ
6. Starting RabbitMQ Server
7. Enabling web management plugin
8. Web Management plugin
9. Conclusion

What is Erlang

Erlang is a general-purpose programming language and runtime environment.

Erlang has built-in support for concurrency, distribution and fault tolerance. Erlang is used in several large telecommunication systems from Ericsson.

Referred from: - http://erlang.org/faq/introduction.html

Link to download Erlang

http://www.erlang.org/downloads

After downloading Erlang now, we are going to Installing Erlang.

Installing Erlang

In this part just click on Erlang setup which you have downloaded to install.

After downloading Erlang setup just install it, after installing next we are going to Download RabbitMQ.

Downloading RabbitMQ

First, we are going to download RabbitMQ setup for windows from link

https://www.rabbitmq.com/download.html

Downloading and Installing RabbitMQ

The latest release of RabbitMQ is **3.7.7**. For release notes, see changelog.

RabbitMQ Server

Installation guides

Linux, BSD, UNIX: Debian, Ubuntu | RHEL, CentOS, Fedora | Generic Unix | Solaris
Windows: With installer (recommended) | Manual
MacOS: Homebrew | Standalone | Generic Unix
Erlang/OTP for RabbitMQ

After downloading RabbitMQ now we are going to Installing RabbitMQ

Installing RabbitMQ

In this part just click on RabbitMQ setup which you have downloaded to install.

After installing Rabbit MQ Next, search RabbitMQ Command Prompt and open it with admin privilege.

Starting RabbitMQ Server

In this part we are going to open RabbitMQ Command Prompt with admin privileges for checking status of RabbitMQ server.

After opening command prompt enter command **"rabbitmqctl status"** for checking status of RabbitMQ server. If it shows you an error as below snapshot then you need to follow some step given below.

```
Administrator: RabbitMQ Command Prompt (sbin dir)

C:\Program Files\RabbitMQ Server\rabbitmq_server-3.7.7\sbin>rabbitmqctl status
Status of node rabbit@Sai-PC ...
Error: unable to perform an operation on node 'rabbit@Sai-PC'. Please see diagno
stics information and suggestions below.

Most common reasons for this are:

 * Target node is unreachable (e.g. due to hostname resolution, TCP connection o
r firewall issues)
 * CLI tool fails to authenticate with the server (e.g. due to CLI tool's Erlang
 cookie not matching that of the server)
 * Target node is not running

In addition to the diagnostics info below:

 * See the CLI, clustering and networking guides on http://rabbitmq.com/document
ation.html to learn more
 * Consult server logs on node rabbit@Sai-PC

DIAGNOSTICS
===========

attempted to contact: ['rabbit@Sai-PC']
```

Steps if you get Error (Authentication failed (rejected by the remote node), check the Erlang cookie)

1. In File Explorer navigate to your user directory. (Paste %userprofile% in the address bar.)
2. If you already have the file .erlang.cookie in there, delete it. If not, just go to the next step.
3. In a second File Explorer, navigate to C:\Windows\System32\config\systemprofile.
4. Find the file. erlang.cookie and copy it to your user directory.
5. Now your rabbitmqctl should be able to authenticate.

Links for Solution

- https://stackoverflow.com/questions/47893899/authentication-failed-rejected-by-the-remote-node-please-check-the-erlang-coo?rq=1
- https://stackoverflow.com/questions/28258392/rabbitmq-has-nodedown-error

After you completed steps again if you running the same command **"rabbitmqctl status"** then below screen should appear.

```
Administrator: RabbitMQ Command Prompt (sbin dir)

C:\Program Files\RabbitMQ Server\rabbitmq_server-3.7.7\sbin>rabbitmqctl status
Status of node rabbit@Sai-PC ...
[{pid,8492},
 {running_applications,
     [{rabbit_common,
          "Modules shared by rabbitmq-server and rabbitmq-erlang-client",
          "3.7.7"},
      {ranch_proxy_protocol,"Ranch Proxy Protocol Transport","1.5.0"},
      {ranch,"Socket acceptor pool for TCP protocols.","1.5.0"},
      {ssl,"Erlang/OTP SSL application","8.2.4"},
      {public_key,"Public key infrastructure","1.5.2"},
      {asn1,"The Erlang ASN1 compiler version 5.0.5","5.0.5"},
      {inets,"INETS  CXC 138 49","6.5"},
      {recon,"Diagnostic tools for production use","2.3.2"},
      {xmerl,"XML parser","1.3.16"},
      {os_mon,"CPO  CXC 138 46","2.4.4"},
      {jsx,"a streaming, evented json parsing toolkit","2.8.2"},
      {cowlib,"Support library for manipulating Web protocols.","2.1.0"},
      {crypto,"CRYPTO","4.2.1"},
      {mnesia,"MNESIA  CXC 138 12","4.15.3"},
      {lager,"Erlang logging framework","3.6.3"},
      {goldrush,"Erlang event stream processor","0.1.9"},
      {compiler,"ERTS  CXC 138 10","7.1.5"},
      {syntax_tools,"Syntax tools","2.1.4"},
```

Now we have started Server next we are going to enable web management plugin of RabbitMQ.

Enabling web management plugin

For enabling web management plugin, you need to start RabbitMQ command prompt with administrator privilege and enter the command "**rabbitmq-plugins enable rabbitmq_management**".

After executing this command, you will see below plugins will be enabled.

```
The following plugins have been enabled:
  mochiweb
  webmachine
  rabbitmq_web_dispatch
  amqp_client
  rabbitmq_management_agent
  rabbitmq_management
```

This screen is same but I have already enabled plugin that's why it is should different messages.

```
Administrator: RabbitMQ Command Prompt (sbin dir)

C:\Program Files\RabbitMQ Server\rabbitmq_server-3.7.7\sbin>rabbitmq-plugins ena
ble rabbitmq_management
Enabling plugins on node rabbit@Sai-PC:
rabbitmq_management
The following plugins have been configured:
  rabbitmq_management
  rabbitmq_management_agent
  rabbitmq_web_dispatch
Applying plugin configuration to rabbit@Sai-PC...
Plugin configuration unchanged.

C:\Program Files\RabbitMQ Server\rabbitmq_server-3.7.7\sbin>
```

Now you can open web management plugin in the browser.

Web Management plugin

Now to use web Management plugin enter localhost URL in browser "http://localhost:15672/".

After entering localhost URL in browser, it will ask for credentials for accessing web management plugin.

The Default Username and password of management plugin is "guest" (Username: "guest" | Password: "guest").

After login with default credentials below overview screen will appear.

For detail information on all tabs, you can visit: - https://www.cloudamqp.com/blog/2015-05-27-part3-rabbitmq-for-beginners_the-management-interface.html#overview

RabbitMQ Exchanges

What are the Exchanges?

When a producer creates a message, it is not directly sent to a queue first message is send to exchanges after that a routing agent reads and sends it to the appropriate queue with help of header attributes, bindings, and routing keys. There are four types of Exchanges which route the message in different ways along with that there are various parameters which you can set such as Type, Durability Auto-delete, Internal,

Direct Exchange

Direct: A direct exchange delivers messages to queues based on a message routing key. In a direct exchange, the message is routed to the queues whose binding key exactly matches the routing key of the message.

Fanout Exchange

Fanout: A fanout exchange routes messages to all of the queues that are bound to it.

Topic Exchange

Topic: The topic exchange does a wildcard match between the routing key and the routing pattern specified in the binding.

Headers Exchange

Headers: Headers exchanges use the message header attributes for routing.

Properties Details

Name

The name will be an exchange name which you will set it must be unique.

Type

Direct: A direct exchange delivers messages to queues based on a message routing key. In a direct exchange, the message is routed to the queues whose binding key exactly matches the routing key of the message.

Fanout: A fanout exchange routes messages to all of the queues that are bound to it.

Topic: The topic exchange does a wildcard match between the routing key and the routing pattern specified in the binding.

Headers: Headers exchanges use the message header attributes for routing.

Durability

Durability is a property of exchange which tells that a message can survive server restarts (broker restart).

There are 2 types of Durability options.

1. Durable
2. Transient (Non-Durable)

Durable: - if you mark exchange as durable then it will survive server restarts

Transient: - if you mark exchange as Transient then it will not survive server restarts.

Auto delete

There are 2 options in auto delete

1. Yes
2. No

If yes, the exchange will delete itself after at least one queue or exchange has been bound to this one, and then all queues or exchanges have been unbound.

e.g. In this part, if you Create an Exchange and bind it to a queue and as you unbind queue it will delete it exchange also.

Internal

If set, the exchange may not be used directly by publishers, but only when bound to other exchanges. Internal exchanges are used to construct wiring that is not visible to applications.

Alternate-exchange:

If there is an issue in publishing message to an exchange you can specify alternate exchange it will send a message to another queue.

Adding Exchanges

To add exchanges, we are first going to log in with default credentials and then we are going to choose Exchanges tab.

After choosing tab you will see "Add a new exchange panel" just click on that panel to expand, next after expansion it will ask for exchange name for demo we are going to name exchange as "**demoexchange**" and in type we are going to choose "direct" and click on add button to create.

After entering all details next, we are going click on add exchange button to create an exchange.

Snapshot after adding Exchanges

amq.direct	direct	D
amq.fanout	fanout	D
amq.headers	headers	D
amq.match	headers	D
amq.rabbitmq.trace	topic	D I
amq.topic	topic	D
demoexchange	direct	D

In a similar way, we can add various exchanges and with different types.

RabbitMQ Queues

What is the Queue?

A Queue is a Buffer that stores messages that are sent from exchanges to queues.

Parameters of Queues in details

Name

Name of the queue which we can reference in the application. The name must be unique and it must not be any system define queue name.

Durability

Durability is a property of queue which tells that a message can survive server restarts (broker restart).

There are 2 types of Durability options.

1. Durable
2. Transient (Non-Durable)

Durable: - if you mark queue as durable then it will survive server restarts

Transient: - if you mark exchange as Transient then it will not survive server restarts.

[Screenshot: Add a new queue form with Durability dropdown showing Durable/Transient options, Auto delete field, Arguments field, and options for Message TTL, Auto expire, Max length, Max length bytes, Dead letter exchange, Dead letter routing key, Maximum priority, Lazy mode, Master locator. Add queue button below.]

Auto delete

There are 2 options in auto delete

1. Yes
2. No

If the queue is exclusive, the durability attribute has no effect because the queue will be deleted as soon as client disconnects (or its connection is lost). auto-deleted queues are deleted when the last consumer is canceled (or its channel is closed, or its connection is lost).

If there never was a consumer it won't be deleted.

Arguments

Arguments (optional; used by plugins and broker-specific features such as message TTL, queue length limit, etc)

Time-to-live

In this part, you can set timespan to a queue which will discard if it reaches its lifespan which is set.

Time will be in milliseconds.

[Screenshot: Add a new queue form filled with Name: demo, Durability: Durable, Auto delete: No, Arguments: x-message-ttl = 120000 Number. Note indicates "1 Minute = 60000 Milliseconds". Add queue button below.]

Auto expire

In this part, you can set expiry to a queue by setting this property.

This controls for how long a queue can be unused before it is automatically deleted.

Unused means the queue has no consumers, the queue has not been redeclared, and basic.get has not been invoked for a duration of at least the expiration period

Max Length

How many (ready) messages a queue can contain before it starts to drop them from its head.

A maximum number of messages can be set by supplying the x-max-length queue declaration argument with a non-negative integer value.

e.g. If you set value x-max-length = 2 and if you publish 3 messages in the queue then only 2 messages will be there the oldest will be deleted from the queue.

Add a new queue

Name:	[ ] *
Durability:	Durable ▼
Auto delete: ?	No ▼
Arguments:	`x-max-length` = `10` Number ▼
	[ ] = [ ] String ▼

Add   Message TTL ? | Auto expire ? | Max length ? | Max length bytes ? |
Dead letter exchange ? | Dead letter routing key ? | Maximum priority ?
Lazy mode ? Master locator ?

[Add queue]

Max Length Bytes

Total body size for ready messages a queue can contain before it starts to drop them from its head.

Maximum length in bytes can be set by supplying the x-max-length-bytes queue declaration argument with a non-negative integer value.

(Sets the "x-max-length-bytes" argument.) 1000000 bytes = 1MB

e.g. If you set value x-max-length-bytes = 1000000 and if you publish messages in queue and the queue size increase more than 1 MB then the oldest will be deleted from the queue (drop them from its head).

Add a new queue

Name:	`demoqueue` *
Durability:	Durable ▼
Auto delete: ?	No ▼
Arguments:	`x-max-length-bytes` = `1000000` Number ▼
	[ ] = [ ] String ▼

Add   Message TTL ? | Auto expire ? | Max length ? | Max length bytes ? |
Dead letter exchange ? | Dead letter routing key ? | Maximum priority
Lazy mode ? Master locator ?

[Add queue]

Overflow behaviour

Sets the queue overflow behavior. This determines what happens to messages when the maximum length of a queue is reached. Valid values are drop-head or reject-publish.

Add a new queue

Name:	[ ] *
Durability:	Durable ▼
Auto delete: ?	No ▼
Arguments:	x-overflow = drop-head String ▼
	[ ] = [ ] String ▼

Add Message TTL ? | Auto expire ? | Max length ? | Max length bytes ? |
Dead letter exchange ? | Dead letter routing key ? | Maximum priority ?
Lazy mode ? | Master locator ?

[Add queue]

Dead letter exchange

Optional name of an exchange to which messages will be republished if they are rejected or expire.

Add a new queue

Name:	[ ] *
Durability:	Durable ▼
Auto delete: ?	No ▼
Arguments:	x-dead-letter-exchange = defaultexchange String ▼
	[ ] = [ ] String ▼

Add Message TTL ? | Auto expire ? | Max length ? | Max length bytes ? |
Dead letter exchange ? | Dead letter routing key ? | Maximum priority ?
Lazy mode ? | Master locator ?

[Add queue]

Dead letter routing key

Optional replacement routing key to use when a message is dead-lettered. If this is not set, the message's original routing key will be used.

For example, if you publish a message to an exchange with routing key foo, and that message is dead-lettered, it will be published to its dead letter exchange with routing key foo. If the queue the message originally landed on had been declared with x-dead-letter-routing-key set to bar, then the message will be published to its dead letter exchange with routing key bar.

Add a new queue

[Form screenshot: Name, Durability: Durable, Auto delete: No, Arguments: x-dead-letter-routing-key = demokey (String). Add | Message TTL | Auto expire | Max length | Max length bytes | Dead letter exchange | Dead letter routing key | Maximum priority | Lazy mode | Master locator. Add queue button.]

Maximum priority

A maximum number of priority levels for the queue to support; if not set, the queue will not support message priorities.

(Sets the "x-max-priority" argument.)

To declare a priority queue, use the x-max-priority optional queue argument. This argument should be a positive integer between 1 and 255, indicating the maximum priority the queue should support

[Form screenshot: Name, Durability: Durable, Auto delete: No, Arguments: x-max-priority = 1 (Number). Add | Message TTL | Auto expire | Max length | Max length bytes | Dead letter exchange | Dead letter routing key | Maximum priority | Lazy mode | Master locator. Add queue button.]

Lazy mode

Set the queue into the lazy mode, keeping as many messages as possible on disk to reduce RAM usage; if not set, the queue will keep an in-memory cache to deliver messages as fast as possible.

(Sets the "x-queue-mode" argument.)

Master locator

Set the queue into master location mode, determining the rule by which the queue master is located when declared on a cluster of nodes.

(Sets the "x-queue-master-locator" argument.)

Adding queue

To create a queue, you need to click on the queue tab in web management plugin.

After clicking on queues tab, you will see add Queue panel with an arrow just click on that panel to expand.

Queues

[RabbitMQ interface screenshot showing the Queues tab with "All queues (0)", pagination, "... no queues ...", and an "Add a new queue" panel]

After clicking on Add a new panel queue will expand in that we are going enter queue details.

First, we are going to start with the name of the queue we are going to name it as **"demoqueue"** then we are going to choose durability as a Durable and final option we are going set is auto delete to No and click on Add queue button to create a queue.

[Screenshot of "Add a new queue" form with Name: demoqueue, Durability: Durable, Auto delete: No, Arguments fields, and an Add queue button]

After adding a queue, you can view queue which you have recently added, it is located just above add queue panel.

Queues

▼ **All queues (1)**

Pagination

Page `1 ▼` of 1 - Filter: [   ]   ☐ Regex ?

Overview			Messages			Message rates			+/-
Name	Features	State	Ready	Unacked	Total	incoming	deliver / get	ack	
demoqueue	D	idle	0	0	0				

Binding in RabbitMQ

What is Binding

A binding is a connection which we can configure between a queue and an exchange.

Simple words: - A binding is a relationship between an exchange and a queue.

In this part, we are going to bind exchange with queue using routing key and this will be used for direct type exchange. The exchange will route the request to particular queue on basis of routing key.

For binding click on queue name which you have entered "**demoqueue**" after click on it bindings panel will expand, next it will ask for exchange name enter exchange name which we have created "**demoexchange**" and routing key "**demokey**" and click on bind button.

Snapshot after binding

Bindings

From	Routing key	Arguments	
(Default exchange binding)			
demoexchange	demokey		Unbind

⇓

This queue

After binding if you want to unbind it then you can click on unbind button to remove binding.

RabbitMQ Users

In this part, we are going to learn how to create a new User and give permission to New User.

For creating a New user, we need to login into Web Management Plugin using default credentials.

After logging into the application, we are going to choose Admin tab.

After choosing admin tab we can see a default user which is "**guest**" which as "administrator" privilege below that we can see add new user panel.

Clicking on "Add a User" panel to create new Users.

```
▼ Add a user
      Username: [        ] *
                          *
Password: ▼   [        ]
              [        ] * (confirm)
         Tags: [        ] ?
               Set  Admin | Monitoring | Policymaker
                    Management | Impersonator | None

[Add user]
```

Before moving ahead lets first have a look at tags. Tags in this part are as rights (privileges) which are assigned to users which are created. we can set single or multiple privileges to a user if we want multiple privileges then just set privileges as comma-separated (administrator, management)

Currently supported by the management plugin

Management

The user can access the management plugin

Policymaker

The user can access the management plugin and manage policies and parameters for the vhosts they have access to.

Monitoring

The user can access the management plugin and see all connections and channels as well as node-related information.

Administrator

The user can do everything monitoring can do, manage users, vhosts, and permissions, close other user's connections, and manage policies and parameters for all vhosts.

Creating Users

In this part we are going to create new user and we are going to set Username as "**demouser**" after that we are going to set password as "123456" after that we are going set privilege to this user as "**administrator**" (just click on Admin link it will set "**administrator**" in tags field) finally click on Add user to create new user.

▼ **Add a user**

Username:	demouser	*
Password: ▼	••••••	*
	••••••	* (confirm)
Tags:	administrator	?
	Set **Admin** | **Monitoring** | **Policymaker** **Management** | **Impersonator** | **None**	

Add user

After adding a user, you can see all Users in all user's panel just expand it. After expanding you can see the new user "demouser" but in the grid, you can see "can access virtual hosts" columns where it has the value "No access" which means we do not have the privilege to virtual hosts.

Users

▼ **All users**

Filter: [   ] ☐ Regex ?

Name	Tags	Can access virtual hosts	Has password
demouser	administrator	No access	•
guest	administrator	/	•

?

Setting privilege to access virtual hosts

For setting permission just click on username which we have created "demouser".

Name	Tags	Can access virtual hosts	Has password
demouser	administrator	No access	●
guest	administrator	/	●

After clicking on "**demouser**" go to permission panel which is just below overview panel.

Just expand permission panel and just click on set permission button to set permission to demouser.

Once the permission is set, you'll see the "Current permission" as shown below.

Now you should be able to log in as this "**demouser**" to the RabbitMQ Web Management Plugin.

User: demouser

Overview

Tags: administrator
Can log in with password: ●

Permissions

Current permissions

Virtual host	Configure regexp	Write regexp	Read regexp
/	.*	.*	.*

Let's login into RabbitMQ Web Management Plugin with new user "demouser".

Below is snapshot after logging into RabbitMQ Web Management Plugin with new user "demouser".

RabbitMQ Virtual Hosts

What are Virtual Hosts?

Virtual hosts are like a virtual box which contains a logical grouping of connections, exchanges, queues, bindings, user permissions, policies and many more things.

We can create different virtual host and each virtual host will have users.

Creating Virtual host

To create a new virtual host, we are first going to log in with default credentials and then we are going to choose admin tab.

After choosing admin tab you will see vertical menus in right part of the page in that choose "**Virtual Hosts**".

After choosing "**Virtual Hosts**" you will see the default "**Virtual Hosts**" which is already present below that there is a panel "**Add a new virtual host**" just click on it to expand.

After expanding we can see for adding virtual host we need to add Name parameter here I am entering the name as "**demohost**" next click on Add virtual host button to create "**demohost**" virtual host.

After adding a virtual host, we can see the newly added virtual host in All virtual hosts panel.

Now till now, we have created virtual host but we have not assigned any user to this virtual host let's create new User.

Creating Users

In this part we are going to create new user and we are going to set Username as "**virtualuser**" after that we are going to set password as "123456" after that we are going set privilege to this user as "**administrator**" (just click on Admin link it will set "**administrator**" in tags field) finally click on Add user to create new user.

After adding a user, you can see all Users in all user's panel just expand it. After expanding you can see the new user "**virtualuser**" but in the grid, you can see "can access virtual hosts" columns where it has the value "No access" which means we do not have the privilege to virtual hosts.

Setting privilege to access virtual hosts

For setting permission just click on username which we have created "**virtualuser**".

After clicking on "**virtualuser**" go to permission panel which is just below overview panel.

32 | Page

Just expand permission panel and just click on set permission button to set permission to **virtualuser**.

▼ Permissions

Current permissions

... no permissions ...

Set permission

Virtual Host:	demohost ▼
Configure regexp:	.*
Write regexp:	.*
Read regexp:	.*

Set permission

The default value is ".*" which allows access to all exchanges and queues in the virtual host.

Once the permission is set, you'll see the "Current permission" as shown below.

User: virtualuser

▼ Overview

Tags	administrator
Can log in with password	•

▼ Permissions

Current permissions

Virtual host	Configure regexp	Write regexp	Read regexp	
demohost	.*	.*	.*	Clear

Now you should be able to log in as this "**virtualuser**" to the RabbitMQ Web Management Plugin.

Let's login into RabbitMQ Web Management Plugin with new user "**virtualuser**".

Below is snapshot after logging into RabbitMQ Web Management Plugin with new user "**virtualuser**".

Now we have completed creating new virtual host along with that we have to assign a new user to it.

Connections

A connection is a TCP connection between your application and the RabbitMQ broker.

Referenced from: - https://www.cloudamqp.com/blog/2015-05-18-part1-rabbitmq-for-beginners-what-is-rabbitmq.html

In connection tab it will show live connections of both producer of message and consumer of the message along with that it will show usernames of each connection with the state of connection if you are using SSL/TLS then it will indicate in the connection it will mark with a dark dot "." It will also show which protocol is been used after that in the network it will show from the client and to client network utilization.

RabbitMQ 3.7.5 Erlang 20.3

Overview | **Connections** | Channels | Exchanges | Queues | Admin

Connections
▼ All connections (15)

Pagination

Page 1 ▼ of 1 - Filter: [   ] ☐ Regex ?

Overview			Details			Network	
Name	User name	State	SSL / TLS	Protocol	Channels	From client	To client
[::1]:53662 undefined	guest	running	○	AMQP 0-9-1	1	0B/s	0B/s
[::1]:53671 undefined	guest	running	○	AMQP 0-9-1	1	0B/s	0B/s
[::1]:53672 undefined	guest	running	○	AMQP 0-9-1	1	0B/s	0B/s
[::1]:53673 undefined	guest	running	○	AMQP 0-9-1	1	0B/s	0B/s
[::1]:53674 undefined	guest	running	○	AMQP 0-9-1	1	0B/s	0B/s

If you want to see details of each connection then click on connection name.

Connections
▼ All connections (6)

Pagination

Page 1 ▼ of 1 - Filter: [   ] ☐ Regex ?

Overview			Details			Network	
Name	User name	State	SSL / TLS	Protocol	Channels	▼ From client	To client
[::1]:54708 undefined	guest	running	○	AMQP 0-9-1	1	2B/s	2B/s

After clicking on connection name, it will show all details of connection along with data rates, channels, client properties, runtime metric, and finally close connection.

If you want to close connection then you can open "close this connection" tab type reason and click on force close button.

Channels

A channel is a virtual connection inside a connection. When you are publishing or consuming messages from a queue - it's all done over a channel.

Referenced from: - https://www.cloudamqp.com/blog/2015-05-18-part1-rabbitmq-for-beginners-what-is-rabbitmq.html

In channel tab it will show live channels of both producer of message and consumer of the message along with that it will show mode. There are 2 modes. C – confirm Channel will send streaming publish confirmations. T – transactional Channel is transactional after that it will show state of channel. Next details in that we have Unconfirmed column it will show Number of published messages not yet confirmed next to Unconfirmed column is Prefetch column which shows details of per channel limit. Next to Prefetch column is Unacked column the Unacked means that the consumer has promised to process them but has not acknowledged that they are processed further we have message rates which show published and confirmed rates along with delivered and acknowledge details.

Note for Mode

Channel guarantee mode. Can be one of the following, or neither:

C – confirm

Channel will send streaming publish confirmations.

T – transactional

Channel is transactional.

Note for Prefetch count

Channel prefetch counts.

Each channel can have two prefetch counts: A per-consumer count, which will limit each new consumer created on the channel, and a global count, which is shared between all consumers on the channel.

This column shows one, the other, or both limits if they are set.

Overview				Details			Message rates			
Channel	User name	Mode ?	State	Unconfirmed	Prefetch ?	Unacked	publish	confirm	deliver / get	ack
[::1]:56857 (1)	guest		idle	0		0	0.00/s	0.00/s		
[::1]:56856 (1)	guest		idle	0		0	0.00/s	0.00/s		
[::1]:56855 (1)	guest		idle	0		0	0.00/s	0.00/s		
[::1]:56854 (1)	guest		idle	0		0	0.00/s	0.00/s		
[::1]:56853 (1)	guest		idle	0		0	0.00/s	0.00/s		

If you want to see details of each channel then click on "channel" name "[::1]:57086 (1)" it will show all details related to that channel.

| Overview | Connections | **Channels** | Exchanges | Queues | Admin |

Channel: [::1]:57086 -> [::1]:5672 (1)
▼ Overview

Message rates last minute ?

```
1.0/s
0.0/s
  15:40:50  15:41:00  15:41:10  15:41:20  15:41:30  15:41:40
```

Publish	■ 0.00/s
Publisher confirm	■ 0.00/s
Return	■ 0.00/s

Details

Connection	[::1]:57086	State	idle	Messages unacknowledged	0
Username	guest	Prefetch count	0	Messages unconfirmed	0
Mode ?		Global prefetch count	0	Messages uncommitted	0
				Acks uncommitted	0

▼ Consumers

... no consumers ...

▶ Runtime Metrics (Advanced)

Publishing Message

For publishing a message Login into web management plugin with credentials.

After logging into web management plugin next click on the queue(demoqueue).

Queues
▼ All queues (1)

Pagination

Page 1 ▼ of 1 - Filter: [   ] ☐ Regex ?

Overview			Messages			Message rates			+/-
Name	Features	State	Ready	Unacked	Total	incoming	deliver / get	ack	
demoqueue	D	idle	10	0	10	0.00/s	0.00/s	0.00/s	

After clicking on demoqueue "queue" just Below bindings panel is publish message panel in that just enter a message in Payload text area and click on publish message.

| Overview | Connections | Channels | Exchanges | **Queues** | Admin |

Process memory ?   14kB

▶ Consumers

▶ Bindings

▶ **Publish message**

▶ Get messages

▼ Publish message

Message will be published to the default exchange with routing key **demoqueue**, routing it to this queue.

Delivery mode: [1 - Non-persistent ▼]

Headers: ? [   ] = [   ] [String ▼]

Properties: ? [   ] = [   ]

Payload: Hello RabbitMQ

[Publish message]

Snapshot after publishing message

39 | Page

Arguments:

Message published.

Bind

Close

▼ **Publish message**

Message will be published to the default exchange with routing key **demoqueue**, routing it to this queue.

Delivery mode: | 1 - Non-persistent ▼

Headers: ? [   ] = [   ] String ▼

Properties: ? [   ] = [   ]

Payload: Hello RabbitMQ

Publish message

Reading Message

For reading a message Login into web management plugin with credentials.

After logging into web management plugin next click on the queue(demoqueue).

40 | Page

Queues
▼ All queues (1)

Pagination

Page 1 ▼ of 1 - Filter: [   ] ☐ Regex ?

Overview			Messages			Message rates			+/-
Name	Features	State	Ready	Unacked	Total	incoming	deliver / get	ack	
demoqueue	D	idle	10	0	10	0.00/s	0.00/s	0.00/s	

Below publishes message is Get message here you can read a message from "**demoqueue**" here in message textbox you can enter the count of messages to read from the queue and click on Get Message but to get Message.

Overview   Connections   Channels   Exchanges   **Queues**   Admin

Process memory ? | 14kB

▶ Consumers

▶ Bindings

▶ Publish message

▶ Get messages

▼ Get messages

Warning: getting messages from a queue is a destructive action. ?

Ack Mode: [Nack message requeue true ▼]
Encoding: [Auto string / base64 ▼] ?
Messages: [1]

[Get Message(s)]

Snapshot while reading the message

41 | P a g e

▼ **Get messages**

Warning: getting messages from a queue is a destructive action. ?

Ack Mode: | Nack message requeue true ▼
Encoding: | Auto string / base64 ▼ | ?
Messages: | 1

[Get Message(s)]

Message 1

The server reported 1 messages remaining.

Exchange	(AMQP default)
Routing Key	demoqueue
Redelivered	●
Properties	delivery_mode: 1
	headers:
Payload 14 bytes Encoding: string	Hello RabbitMQ

After reading the message next last part we are going to see is Deleting Queue.

Delete Message

For deleting a message Login into web management plugin with credentials.

After logging into web management plugin next click on the queue(demoqueue).

To delete the message, you can expand delete panel in that you will see only delete button. Just click on it to delete.

Overview	Connections	Channels	Exchanges	Queues	Admin

Process memory ? 14kB

▶ **Consumers**

▶ **Bindings**

▶ **Publish message**

▶ **Get messages**

▶ **Move messages**

▶ **Delete**

▼ Delete

Delete Queue

After clicking on deleting a message it will ask for confirmation as shown below.

If we click on the ok button it will delete queue.

Publish Message Using C# to RabbitMQ

In this article, we are going to learn how to Publish a Message to RabbitMQ using .Net Application and RabbitMQ.Client in step by step way.

Creating RequestRabbitMQ Application

Let's Create a simple console application with Name "**RequestRabbitMQ**".

After creating application next we are going to add "**RabbitMQ.Client**" NuGet package.

Adding RabbitMQ.Client NuGet Package

In this part for creating a connection with the RabbitMQ server to create request, we need to add "RabbitMQ.Client" package from NuGet Package.

Command to install: - Install-Package RabbitMQ.Client -Version 5.1.0

After installing NuGet package of "**RabbitMQ.Client**" next we are going to create an exchange from web admin console.

Adding Direct Exchange

In this part, we are going to create an exchange for doing that we have first created a connection to RabbitMQ server using RabbitMQ.Client after creating connection next we have passed credentials along with HostName to connectionFactory after that we have created a connection by calling "**CreateConnection**" method, next to add exchange we have called method "**ExchangeDeclare**" method and passed parameters such as "exchange name" and "exchange type".

Code Snippet

```
using RabbitMQ.Client;
```

```csharp
using System;

namespace RequestRabbitMQ
{
    class Program
    {
        static void Main(string[] args)
        {
            string UserName = "guest";
            string Password = "guest";
            string HostName = "localhost";

            //Main entry point to the RabbitMQ .NET AMQP client
            var connectionFactory = new RabbitMQ.Client.ConnectionFactory()
            {
                UserName = UserName,
                Password = Password,
                HostName = HostName
            };

            var connection = connectionFactory.CreateConnection();
            var model = connection.CreateModel();

            //// Create Exchange
            model.ExchangeDeclare("demoExchange", ExchangeType.Direct);

            Console.ReadLine();
        }
    }
}
```

Let's check result by running application.

```
Creating Exchange
```

After adding exchange let's check web management plugin you will see we have successfully created exchanges.

Overview	Connections	Channels	Exchanges	Queues	Admin
amq.direct	direct	D			
amq.fanout	fanout	D			
amq.headers	headers	D			
amq.match	headers	D			
amq.rabbitmq.trace	topic	D I			
amq.topic	topic	D			
demoExchange	direct				

Adding queue

Now we are going to add a queue.

For doing that we are going to add call "**QueueDeclare**" method and pass parameters to it.

Method definition

```
//
// Summary:
//     Declare a queue.
[AmqpMethodDoNotImplement(null)]
QueueDeclareOk QueueDeclare(string queue, bool durable, bool exclusive, bool autoDelete, IDictionary<string, object> arguments);
//
```

First parameter is queue name "demoqueue".

The second parameter is Durable "true".

The third parameter is Exclusive "false".

The fourth parameter is autodelete "false".

Fifth parameter is Arguments "null".

```
// Create Queue
model.QueueDeclare("demoqueue", true, false, false, null);
```

Code Snippet

```csharp
using RabbitMQ.Client;
using System;

namespace RequestRabbitMQ
{
    class Program
    {
        static void Main(string[] args)
        {
            string UserName = "guest";
            string Password = "guest";
            string HostName = "localhost";

            //Main entry point to the RabbitMQ .NET AMQP client
            var connectionFactory = new RabbitMQ.Client.ConnectionFactory()
            {
                UserName = UserName,
                Password = Password,
                HostName = HostName
            };

            var connection = connectionFactory.CreateConnection();
            var model = connection.CreateModel();

            //// Create Exchange
            //model.ExchangeDeclare("demoExchange", ExchangeType.Direct);
            //Console.WriteLine("Creating Exchange");
```

```
            // Create Queue
            model.QueueDeclare("demoqueue", true, false, false, null);
            Console.WriteLine("Creating Queue");

            Console.ReadLine();
        }
    }
}
```

Let's check result by running application.

```
file:///H:/RabbitMQApps/Publish/RequestRabbitMQ/RequestRabbitMQ/bin/Debug/RequestRabbit...
Creating Queue
```

After adding queue let's check web management plugin you will see we have successfully created the queue.

Queues
▼ All queues (1)

Pagination

Page 1 ▼ of 1 - Filter: [   ]   ☐ Regex ?

Overview			Messages			Message rates			+/-
Name	Features	State	Ready	Unacked	Total	incoming	deliver / get	ack	
demoqueue	D	idle	0	0	0				

After adding queue next we are going to bind queue with the exchange.

Binding the demoqueue with demoExchange

In binding, we are going to enter the name of exchange "**demoExchange**" and we are going to enter routing key as "**directexchange_key**".

Method definition

```
//
// Summary:
//     /// (Spec method) Binds a queue. ///
public static void QueueBind(this IModel model, string queue, string exchange, string routingKey, IDictionary<string, object> arguments = null)
//
```

First parameter is queue name "**demoqueue**".

47 | P a g e

The second parameter is Exchange "**demoExchange**".

Third parameter is routing key "**directexchange_key**".

```
// Creating Binding
model.QueueBind("demoqueue", "demoExchange", "directexchange_key");
Console.WriteLine("Creating Binding");
```

Code Snippet

```csharp
using RabbitMQ.Client;
using System;

namespace RequestRabbitMQ
{
    class Program
    {
        static void Main(string[] args)
        {
            string UserName = "guest";
            string Password = "guest";
            string HostName = "localhost";

            //Main entry point to the RabbitMQ .NET AMQP client
            var connectionFactory = new RabbitMQ.Client.ConnectionFactory()
            {
                UserName = UserName,
                Password = Password,
                HostName = HostName
            };

            var connection = connectionFactory.CreateConnection();
            var model = connection.CreateModel();

            //// Create Exchange
            //model.ExchangeDeclare("demoExchange", ExchangeType.Direct);
            //Console.WriteLine("Creating Exchange");

            //// Create Queue
            //model.QueueDeclare("demoqueue", true, false, false, null);
            //Console.WriteLine("Creating Queue");

            // Creating Binding
            model.QueueBind("demoqueue", "demoExchange", "directexchange_key");
            Console.WriteLine("Creating Binding");

            Console.ReadLine();
        }
    }
}
```

After creating binding let's check web management plugin you will see we have successfully created the binding.

	From	Routing key	Arguments	
	(Default exchange binding)			
	demoExchange	directexchange_key		Unbind

⇩

This queue

Now let's Create Push Message to "**demoqueue**" from a console application.

Adding a Directmessages Class

We have created a "Directmessage" name class in this class we are going to create request and push to RabbitMQ.

First, we have declared Username, Password, and HostName as constant. After that, we have created a method with name "**SendMessage**" in that message we have created a connection to RabbitMQ server using RabbitMQ.Client after creating connection next we have passed credentials along with HostName to connectionFactory.

Next, we have written a simple message "Direct Message" and got it in bytes array form, finally, we are going to assign all these values to a BasicPublish method of "**RabbitMQ.Client**"

Method definition

```
/// <summary>
/// (Extension method) Convenience overload of BasicPublish.
/// </summary>
/// <remarks>The publication occurs with mandatory=false</remarks>
public static void BasicPublish(this IModel model, string exchange, string routingKey, IBasicProperties basicProperties, byte[] body
{
    model.BasicPublish(exchange, routingKey, false, basicProperties, body);
}
```

The parameter passed to it

Exchange: "demoExchange"

Routing key: "directexchange_key"

Code Snippet

```csharp
using RabbitMQ.Client;
using System;
using System.Text;

namespace RequestRabbitMQ
{
    class Program
    {
        static void Main(string[] args)
        {
            string UserName = "guest";
            string Password = "guest";
            string HostName = "localhost";

            //Main entry point to the RabbitMQ .NET AMQP client
            var connectionFactory = new RabbitMQ.Client.ConnectionFactory()
            {
                UserName = UserName,
                Password = Password,
                HostName = HostName
            };

            var connection = connectionFactory.CreateConnection();
            var model = connection.CreateModel();

            //// Create Exchange
            //model.ExchangeDeclare("demoExchange", ExchangeType.Direct);
            //Console.WriteLine("Creating Exchange");

            //// Create Queue
            //model.QueueDeclare("demoqueue", true, false, false, null);
            //Console.WriteLine("Creating Queue");

            // Creating Binding
            //model.QueueBind("demoqueue", "demoExchange", "directexchange_key");
            //Console.WriteLine("Creating Binding");

            var properties = model.CreateBasicProperties();
            properties.Persistent = false;

            byte[] messagebuffer = Encoding.Default.GetBytes("Direct Message");

            model.BasicPublish("demoExchange", "directexchange_key", properties, messagebuffer);
            Console.WriteLine("Message Sent");

            Console.ReadLine();
        }
    }
}
```

After completing entire process let's save the application and run after running the application you will see a Message sent a message on a console just for notification.

After sending a message now let's have a look on the queue (demoqueue).

Now Let's See queue status "demoqueue"

If you see Queues status you will see Ready "1" which means we have successfully published a message to "demoqueue".

Queues
▼ All queues (1)

Pagination

Page 1 ▼ of 1 - Filter: [   ]   ☐ Regex ?

Overview			Messages			Message rates			+/-
Name	Features	State	Ready	Unacked	Total	incoming	deliver / get	ack	
demoqueue	D	idle	1	0	1	0.00/s			

Consume Message Using C# to RabbitMQ

In this article we are going to learn how to consume messages from RabbitMQ using .Net in step by step way.

Creating RabbitMQConsumer Application

Let's create another console application for consuming messages from a queue with Name "**RabbitMQConsumer**"

- Solution 'RabbitMQConsumer' (1 project)
  - RabbitMQConsumer
    - Properties
    - References
    - App.config
    - Program.cs

After creating application next we are going to add "**RabbitMQ.Client**" NuGet package.

Adding RabbitMQ.Client NuGet Package

In this part for creating a connection with RabbitMQ server to create request, we need to add "RabbitMQ.Client" package from NuGet Package.

Command to install: - Install-Package RabbitMQ.Client -Version 5.1.0

```
Package Manager Console
Package source: All      Default project: RabbitMQConsumer
Each package is licensed to you by its owner. NuGet is not responsible for, nor does it grant any licenses to,
third-party packages. Some packages may include dependencies which are governed by additional licenses. Follow the
package source (feed) URL to determine any dependencies.

Package Manager Console Host Version 3.4.4.1321

Type 'get-help NuGet' to see all available NuGet commands.

PM> Install-Package RabbitMQ.Client -Version 5.1.0
```

After installing RabbitMQ.Client next we are going to add a class with name "**MessageReceiver**".

Code snippet of MessageReceiver class

In this part, we have created MessageReceiver class and this class inherits DefaultBasicConsumer class which is from RabbitMQ.Client next we have to override HandleBasicDeliver method this method receives message body next, we are going to write these messages as we can see in its console.

```csharp
using System;
using System.Text;
using RabbitMQ.Client;

namespace RabbitMQConsumer
{
    public class MessageReceiver : DefaultBasicConsumer
    {
        private readonly IModel _channel;

        public MessageReceiver(IModel channel)
        {
            _channel = channel;
        }

        public override void HandleBasicDeliver(string consumerTag, ulong deliveryTag, bool redelivered, string exchange, string routingKey, IBasicProperties properties, byte[] body)
        {
            Console.WriteLine($"Consuming Message");
            Console.WriteLine(string.Concat("Message received from the exchange ", exchange));
            Console.WriteLine(string.Concat("Consumer tag: ", consumerTag));
            Console.WriteLine(string.Concat("Delivery tag: ", deliveryTag));
            Console.WriteLine(string.Concat("Routing tag: ", routingKey));
            Console.WriteLine(string.Concat("Message: ", Encoding.UTF8.GetString(body)));
            _channel.BasicAck(deliveryTag, false);
        }
    }
}
```

After completing with understanding code snippet of MessageReceiver class next we are going to calls this class in the Main method.

Code snippet of Main Method

In the main method we have created connectionFactory class and passed credentials and Hostname after that we have created connection, next we have created channel and set prefetchCount to 1 such that it tells RabbitMQ not to give more than one message to a worker at a time, Next, we have created instance of MessageReceiver class and passed IModel (channel) to it, in final step we have called "**BasicConsume**" method and passed queue name to it "**demoqueue**" along with we have set autoAck to false and passed the messageReceiver instance to it.

```csharp
using System;
using System.Collections.Generic;
using System.Linq;
using System.Text;
using System.Threading.Tasks;
using RabbitMQ.Client;

namespace RabbitMQConsumer
{
    class Program
    {
        private const string UserName = "guest";
        private const string Password = "guest";
        private const string HostName = "localhost";

        static void Main(string[] args)
        {
            ConnectionFactory connectionFactory = new ConnectionFactory
            {
                HostName = HostName,
                UserName = UserName,
                Password = Password,
            };

            var connection = connectionFactory.CreateConnection();
            var channel = connection.CreateModel();

            // accept only one unack-ed message at a time
            // uint prefetchSize, ushort prefetchCount, bool global

            channel.BasicQos(0, 1, false);

            MessageReceiver messageReceiver = new MessageReceiver(channel);
            channel.BasicConsume("demoqueue", false, messageReceiver);

            Console.ReadLine();
        }
    }
}
```

Note: - prefetchCount

In order to defeat that we can set the prefetch count with the value of 1. This tells RabbitMQ not to give more than one message to a worker at a time. Or, in other words, don't dispatch a new message to a worker until it has processed and acknowledged the previous one. Instead, it will dispatch it to the next worker that is not still busy.

Now we have complete working mechanism Let's create request from "**RequestRabbitMQ**" console and consume a message from "**RabbitMQConsumer**" application.

Queue is Empty

Queues
▼ All queues (1)

Pagination

Page 1 ▼ of 1 - Filter: [   ] ☐ Regex ?

Overview			Messages			Message rates			+/-
Name	Features	State	Ready	Unacked	Total	incoming	deliver / get	ack	
demoqueue	D	idle	0	0	0	0.00/s	0.00/s	0.00/s	

After we saw that queue (demoqueue) is empty next we are going to publish message to demoqueue.

Publishing Message

```
var connection = connectionFactory.CreateConnection();
var model = connection.CreateModel();

Create Exchange | Create Queue | Creating Binding

var properties = model.CreateBasicProperties();
properties.Persistent = false;

byte[] messagebuffer = Encoding.Default.GetBytes("Direct Message");

model.BasicPublish("demoExchange", "directexchange_key", properties, messagebuffer);
Console.WriteLine("Message Sent");

Console.ReadLine();
```

After we have published message now let's have a view on (queue) demoqueue.

Queue after publishing Message

Queues
▼ All queues (1)

Pagination

Page 1 ▼ of 1 - Filter: [   ] ☐ Regex ?

Overview			Messages			Message rates			+/-
Name	Features	State	Ready	Unacked	Total	incoming	deliver / get	ack	
demoqueue	D	idle	1	0	1	0.00/s	0.00/s	0.00/s	

After we have push message to (queue) demoqueue the console application will start consuming it below is snapshot.

Consumed Message from demoqueue

```
Consuming Message
Message received from the exchange demoExchange
Consumer tag: amq.ctag-ba1aFij02rRYUswC01y31A
Delivery tag: 1
Routing tag: directexchange_key
Message: Direct Message
```

Finally, we have completed consuming Message from RabbitMQ queue.

Using RabbitMQ Direct Message Exchanges with .Net Application

In this article, we are going to use Direct Message Exchanges and push messages into RabbitMQ using .Net Application and RabbitMQ.Client and read messages from RabbitMQ using .Net Application and RabbitMQ.Client in step by step way.

Types of Exchanges

1. Direct

2. fanout

3. Headers

4. Topic

Details of Exchanges

Direct: A direct exchange delivers messages to queues based on a message routing key.

In a direct exchange, the message is routed to the queues whose binding key exactly matches the routing key of the message.

Fanout: A fanout exchange routes messages to all of the queues that are bound to it.

Topic: The topic exchange does a wildcard match between the routing key and the routing pattern specified in the binding.

Headers: Headers exchanges use the message header attributes for routing.

Creating RequestRabbitMQ Application

Let's Create a simple console application with Name "**RequestRabbitMQ**".

After creating application next we are going to add "**RabbitMQ.Client**" NuGet package.

Adding RabbitMQ.Client NuGet Package

In this part for creating a connection with RabbitMQ server to create request, we need to add "RabbitMQ.Client" package from NuGet Package.

Command to install: - Install-Package RabbitMQ.Client -Version 5.1.0

After installing NuGet package of "**RabbitMQ.Client**" next we are going to create an exchange from web admin console.

Adding Direct Exchange

Go to http://localhost:15672/#/exchanges , name exchange as "**request.exchange**" after entering name next, we select Type as "**direct**" and click on add exchange button to create.

After adding exchange (request.exchange) next we are going to add Queue (request Queue).

Adding queue

Go to http://localhost:15672/#/queues , add queue: request.queue.

After adding queue next we are going to bind queue with exchange.

Binding the request.queue with request.exchange

In binding, we are going to enter the name of exchange "**request.exchange**" and we are going to enter routing key as "**directexchange_key**".

Bindings

From	Routing key	Arguments
(Default exchange binding)		
request.exchange	directexchange_key	Unbind

⇓

This queue

Add binding to this queue

From exchange: _____ *
Routing key: _____
Arguments: _____ = _____ String ▼

Bind

Now let's Create Push Message to "**request.queue**" from a console application.

Adding a Directmessages Class

We have created a "Directmessage" name class in this class we are going to create request and push to RabbitMQ.

First, we have declared Username, Password and HostName as constant. After that, we have created a method with name "**SendMessage**" in that message we have created a connection to RabbitMQ server using RabbitMQ.Client after creating connection next we have passed credentials along with HostName to connectionFactory. Next, we have written a simple message "Direct Message" and got it in bytes array form, finally, we are going assign all these values to a BasicPublish method of "**RabbitMQ.Client**"

BasicPublish View

```
/// <summary>
/// (Extension method) Convenience overload of BasicPublish.
/// </summary>
/// <remarks>The publication occurs with mandatory=false</remarks>
public static void BasicPublish(this IModel model, string exchange, string routingKey, IBasicProperties basicProperties, byte[] body)
{
    model.BasicPublish(exchange, routingKey, false, basicProperties, body);
}
```

The parameter passed to it

Exchange: "request.exchange"

Routingkey: "directexchange_key"

Code Snippet

```csharp
using RabbitMQ.Client;
using System.Text;

namespace RequestRabbitMQ
{
    public class Directmessages
    {
        private const string UserName = "guest";
        private const string Password = "guest";
        private const string HostName = "localhost";

        public void SendMessage()
        {
            //Main entry point to the RabbitMQ .NET AMQP client
            var connectionFactory = new RabbitMQ.Client.ConnectionFactory()
            {
                UserName = UserName,
                Password = Password,
                HostName = HostName
            };

            var connection = connectionFactory.CreateConnection();
            var model = connection.CreateModel();

            var properties = model.CreateBasicProperties();
            properties.Persistent = false;


            byte[] messagebuffer = Encoding.Default.GetBytes("Direct Message");

            model.BasicPublish("request.exchange", "directexchange_key", properties, messagebuffer);
            Console.WriteLine("Message Sent");
        }
    }
}
```

Main Code snippet

```csharp
using System;

namespace RequestRabbitMQ
{
    class Program
    {
        static void Main(string[] args)
        {
            Directmessages directmessages = new Directmessages();
            directmessages.SendMessage();
            Console.ReadLine();
        }
    }
}
```

After completing entire process let's save the application and run after running the application you will see a Message sent a message on a console just for notification.

[Console window screenshot: "Message Sent"]

After sending message now let's have a look on queue (request.queue).

Now Let's See queue status "request.queue"

If you see Queues status you will see Ready "1" which means we have successfully published a message to "request.queue".

[Screenshot of RabbitMQ management Queues page showing request.queue with State idle, Ready 1, Unacked 0, Total 1, incoming 0.00/s]

After publishing message next we are going to create .Net Console application for consuming message from queue.

Creating RabbitMQConsumer Application

Let's create another console application for consuming messages from a queue with Name "**RabbitMQConsumer**"

[Screenshot of Solution Explorer showing Solution 'RabbitMQConsumer' (1 project) with RabbitMQConsumer containing Properties, References, App.config, and Program.cs]

After creating application next we are going to add "**RabbitMQ.Client**" NuGet package.

Adding RabbitMQ.Client NuGet Package

In this part for creating a connection with RabbitMQ server to create request, we need to add "RabbitMQ.Client" package from NuGet Package.

Command to install: - Install-Package RabbitMQ.Client -Version 5.1.0

```
Package Manager Console                                                                    ▼ □ X
Package source: All                      ▼  ⚙  Default project: RabbitMQConsumer            ▼  ⇲
Each package is licensed to you by its owner. NuGet is not responsible for, nor does it grant any licenses to,
third-party packages. Some packages may include dependencies which are governed by additional licenses. Follow the
package source (feed) URL to determine any dependencies.

Package Manager Console Host Version 3.4.4.1321

Type 'get-help NuGet' to see all available NuGet commands.

PM> Install-Package RabbitMQ.Client -Version 5.1.0
```

After installing RabbitMQ.Client next we are going to add a class with name "**MessageReceiver**".

Code snippet of MessageReceiver class

In this part, we have created MessageReceiver class and this class inherits DefaultBasicConsumer class which is from RabbitMQ.Client next we have to override HandleBasicDeliver method this method receives message body next, we are going to write these messages as we can see in its console.

```csharp
using System;
using System.Text;
using RabbitMQ.Client;

namespace RabbitMQConsumer
{
    public class MessageReceiver : DefaultBasicConsumer
    {
        private readonly IModel _channel;

        public MessageReceiver(IModel channel)
        {
            _channel = channel;
        }

        public override void HandleBasicDeliver(string consumerTag, ulong deliveryTag, bool redelivered, string exchange, string routingKey, IBasicProperties properties, byte[] body)
        {
            Console.WriteLine($"Consuming Message");
            Console.WriteLine(string.Concat("Message received from the exchange ", exchange));
            Console.WriteLine(string.Concat("Consumer tag: ", consumerTag));
            Console.WriteLine(string.Concat("Delivery tag: ", deliveryTag));
            Console.WriteLine(string.Concat("Routing tag: ", routingKey));
            Console.WriteLine(string.Concat("Message: ", Encoding.UTF8.GetString(body)));
            _channel.BasicAck(deliveryTag, false);
        }
    }
}
```

After completing with understanding code snippet of MessageReceiver class next we are going to calls this class in the Main method.

Code snippet of Main Method

In the main method we have created connectionFactory class and passed credentials and Hostname after that we have created connection, next we have created channel and set prefetchCount to 1 such that it tells RabbitMQ not to give more than one message to a worker at a time, Next, we have created instance of MessageReceiver class and passed IModel (channel) to it, in final step we have called "**BasicConsume**" method and passed queue name to it "**request.queue**" along with we have set autoAck to false and passed the messageReceiver instance to it.

```csharp
using System;
using System.Collections.Generic;
using System.Linq;
using System.Text;
using System.Threading.Tasks;
using RabbitMQ.Client;

namespace RabbitMQConsumer
{
    class Program
    {
        private const string UserName = "guest";
        private const string Password = "guest";
        private const string HostName = "localhost";

        static void Main(string[] args)
        {
            ConnectionFactory connectionFactory = new ConnectionFactory
            {
                HostName = HostName,
                UserName = UserName,
                Password = Password,
            };

            var connection = connectionFactory.CreateConnection();
            var channel = connection.CreateModel();

            // accept only one unack-ed message at a time
            // uint prefetchSize, ushort prefetchCount, bool global

            channel.BasicQos(0, 1, false);

            MessageReceiver messageReceiver = new MessageReceiver(channel);
            channel.BasicConsume("request.queue", false, messageReceiver);

            Console.ReadLine();
        }
    }
}
```

Note: - prefetchCount

In order to defeat that we can set the prefetch count with the value of 1. This tells RabbitMQ not to give more than one message to a worker at a time. Or, in other words, don't dispatch a new message to a worker until it has processed and acknowledged the previous one. Instead, it will dispatch it to the next worker that is not still busy.

Now we have complete working mechanism Let's create request from "**RequestRabbitMQ**" console and consume a message from "**RabbitMQConsumer**" application.

Queue is Empty

Queues
▼ All queues (1)

Pagination

Page 1 ▼ of 1 - Filter: ☐ Regex ?

Overview			Messages			Message rates			+/-
Name	Features	State	Ready	Unacked	Total	incoming	deliver / get	ack	
request.queue	D	idle	0	0	0	0.00/s	0.00/s	0.00/s	

After we saw that queue (request.queue) is empty next we are going to publish message to request.queue.

Publishing Message

```
public class Directmessages
{
    private const string UserName = "guest";
    private const string Password = "guest";
    private const string HostName = "localhost";

    public void SendMessage()
    {
        Code
        byte[] messagebuffer = Encoding.Default.GetBytes("Send My First RabbitMQ Message");

        model.BasicPublish("request.exchange", "directexchange_key", properties, messagebuffer);

        Console.WriteLine("Message Sent");
    }
}
```

After we have published message now let's have a view on (queue) request.queue.

Queue after publishing Message

Exchanges	**Queues**	Admin

Pagination

Page 1 ▼ of 1 - Filter: ☐ Regex ?   Displaying 1 item, page size up to: 100

Overview			Messages			Message rates			+/-
Name	Features	State	Ready	Unacked	Total	incoming	deliver / get	ack	
request.queue	D	idle	1	0	1	0.00/s	0.00/s	0.00/s	

▶ Add a new queue

After we have push message to (queue) request.queue the console application will start consuming it below is snapshot.

Consumed Message from request.queue

```
file:///D:/RabbitMQApp:/RabbitMQConsumer, RabbitMQConsumer/bin/Debug/RabbitMQConsumer.EXE
Consuming Message
Message received from the exchange request.exchange
Consumer tag: amq.ctag-U29QRsqTTkTck1UEHzsugw
Delivery tag: 1
Routing tag: directexchange_key
Message: Send My First RabbitMQ Message
```

Finally, we have completed consuming Message from RabbitMQ queue.

Conclusion

In this article, we have learned how to Produce and consume RabbitMQ Direct Message Exchanges with .Net Application in step by step way along with that how to connect to RabbitMQ server using RabbitMQ.Client, how to create direct exchange, queue and bindings.

Using RabbitMQ Topic Message Exchanges with .Net Application

In this article, we are going to use Topic Message Exchanges and push messages into RabbitMQ using .Net Application and RabbitMQ.Client and read messages from RabbitMQ using .Net Application and RabbitMQ.Client in step by step way.

What is the Topic Exchange?

The topic exchange does a wildcard match between the routing key and the routing pattern specified in the binding.

In topic exchange, the routing key must not be a simple text such as "Bombay" it must be words with delimited by dots such as "*.bombay.*" or "#.bombay" or "Bombay.#".

For example :- I have 2 queues one for Bombay and other for Delhi then the user must send routing key which will match the pattern of routing key then only that message will be added to queue, else message will be lost.

Note: -

* (star) can substitute for exactly one word.

(hash) can substitute for zero or more words.

Creating RequestRabbitMQ Application

Let's Create a simple console application with Name "**RequestRabbitMQ**".

After creating application next we are going to add "**RabbitMQ.Client**" NuGet package.

Adding RabbitMQ.Client NuGet Package

In this part for creating a connection with the RabbitMQ server to create request, we need to add "RabbitMQ.Client" package from NuGet Package.

Command to install: - Install-Package RabbitMQ.Client -Version 5.1.0

After installing NuGet package of "**RabbitMQ.Client**" next we are going to create an exchange from web admin console.

Adding Topic Exchange

Go to http://localhost:15672/#/exchanges , name exchange as "**topic.exchange**" after entering name next, we select Type as "**topic**" and click on add exchange button to create.

After adding "**topic.exchange**" next we are going to Add 2 Queue.

Adding queue

In this part we are going to create 2 queues with different routing key but for same "**topic.exchange**".

Go to http://localhost:15672/#/queues

1. topic.bombay.queue
2. topic.delhi.queue

Adding first queue with name "topic.bombay.queue".

Adding the second queue with name "topic.delhi.queue".

Add a new queue

Name:	topic.delhi.queue *
Durability:	Durable
Auto delete: ?	No
Arguments:	= String

Add Message TTL ? | Auto expire ? | Max length ? | Max length bytes ? |
Dead letter exchange ? | Dead letter routing key ? | Maximum priority
Lazy mode ? Master locator ?

[Add queue]

After adding queue is View of the queues which we have added.

Queues

All queues (3)

Pagination

Page 1 of 1 - Filter: [   ] Regex ?

Overview			Messages			Message rates			+/-
Name	Features	State	Ready	Unacked	Total	incoming	deliver / get	ack	
request.queue	D	idle	0	0	0				
topic.bombay.queue	D	idle	0	0	0				
topic.delhi.queue	D	idle	0	0	0				

After adding queue next we are going to binding queue with "**topic.exchange**".

Binding the topic.bombay.queue with topic.exchange

In this part, we are binding **topic.exchange** with a **topic.bombay.queue** using a pattern of unique routing key "*.Bombay.*".

Add binding to this queue

From exchange: `topic.exchange` *
Routing key: `*.Bombay.*`
Arguments: ▯ = ▯ String ▼

[Bind]

Snapshot of binding

Bindings

From	Routing key	Arguments	
(Default exchange binding)			
topic.exchange	*.Bombay.*		Unbind

⇓

This queue

Binding the topic.delhi.queue with topic.exchange

In this part, we are binding **topic.exchange** with a **topic.delhi.queue** using a pattern of unique routing key "**Delhi.#**".

Add binding to this queue

From exchange: `topic.exchange` *
Routing key: `Delhi.#`
Arguments: ▯ = ▯ String ▼

[Bind]

Snapshot of binding

68 | P a g e

Bindings

From	Routing key	Arguments	
(Default exchange binding)			
topic.exchange	Delhi.#		Unbind

⇓

[This queue]

After completing with binding next we are going to publish message

Adding a Topicmessages Class

we have created a "Topicmessage" name class in this class we are going to create request and push to RabbitMQ.

First, we have declared Username, Password and HostName as constant. After that, we have created a method with name "**SendMessage**" in that message we have created a connection to RabbitMQ server using RabbitMQ.Client after creating connection next we have passed credentials along with HostName to connectionFactory. Next, we have written a simple message "**Message from Topic Exchange 'Bombay'**" and got it in bytes array form, finally, we are going assign all these values to a BasicPublish method of "**RabbitMQ.Client**"

Routing pattern: - "any text .Bombay. any text".

Examples of routing key: -

"Order.Bombay.Pizza",

"Book.Bombay.Hotels",

"Visit.Bombay.Parks",

"List.Bombay.Colleges".

The parameter passed to it

Exchange: "topic.exchange"

Routing key: "Message.Bombay.Email"

Code Snippet

```
public class Topicmessages
{
    private const string UserName = "guest";
    private const string Password = "guest";
    private const string HostName = "localhost";
```

```csharp
    public void SendMessage()
    {
        //Main entry point to the RabbitMQ .NET AMQP client
        var connectionFactory = new RabbitMQ.Client.ConnectionFactory()
        {
            UserName = UserName,Password = Password,HostName = HostName
        };

        var connection = connectionFactory.CreateConnection();
        var model = connection.CreateModel();
        var properties = model.CreateBasicProperties();
        properties.Persistent = false;

   byte[] messagebuffer = Encoding.Default.GetBytes("Message from Topic Exchange 'Bombay' ");
   model.BasicPublish("topic.exchange", "Message.Bombay.Email", properties, messagebuffer);
        Console.WriteLine("Message Sent From :- topic.exchange ");
        Console.WriteLine("Routing Key :- Message.Bombay.Email");
        Console.WriteLine("Message Sent");
    }
}
```

Main Code snippet

```csharp
using System;
namespace RequestRabbitMQ
{
    class Program
    {
        static void Main(string[] args)
        {
            Topicmessages topicmessages = new Topicmessages();
            topicmessages.SendMessage();
            Console.ReadLine();
        }
    }
}
```

After completing entire process let's save the application and run after running the application you will see a Message sent a message on a console just for notification it means we have successfully published a message to "topic.bombay.queue".

Published Message to "topic.bombay.queue"

```
Message Sent From :- topic.exchange
Routing Key :- Message.Bombay.Email
Message Sent
```

Now Let's See queue status "request.queue"

If you see Queues status you will see Ready "1" which means we have successfully published a message to "**topic.bombay.queue**".

Overview			Messages			Message rates			+/-
Name	Features	State	Ready	Unacked	Total	incoming	deliver / get	ack	
request.queue	D	idle	0	0	0				
topic.bombay.queue	D	idle	1	0	1	0.00/s	0.00/s	0.00/s	
topic.delhi.queue	D	idle	0	0	0				

After publishing a message next we are going to create .Net Console application for consuming message from the queue.

Creating RabbitMQConsumer Application

Let's create another console application for consuming messages from a queue with Name "**RabbitMQConsumer**"

```
Solution 'RabbitMQConsumer' (1 project)
  C# RabbitMQConsumer
    ▷ Properties
    ▷ References
        App.config
    ▷ C# Program.cs
```

After creating application next we are going to add "**RabbitMQ.Client**" NuGet package.

Adding RabbitMQ.Client NuGet Package

In this part for creating a connection with the RabbitMQ server to create request, we need to add "RabbitMQ.Client" package from NuGet Package.

Command to install: - Install-Package RabbitMQ.Client -Version 5.1.0

```
Package Manager Console

Package source: All    Default project: RabbitMQConsumer

Each package is licensed to you by its owner. NuGet is not responsible for, nor does it grant any licenses to,
third-party packages. Some packages may include dependencies which are governed by additional licenses. Follow the
package source (feed) URL to determine any dependencies.

Package Manager Console Host Version 3.4.4.1321

Type 'get-help NuGet' to see all available NuGet commands.

PM> Install-Package RabbitMQ.Client -Version 5.1.0
```

After installing RabbitMQ.Client next we are going to add a class with name "**MessageReceiver**".

Code snippet of MessageReceiver class

In this part, we have created MessageReceiver class and this class inherits DefaultBasicConsumer class which is from RabbitMQ.Client next we have to override HandleBasicDeliver method this method receives message body next, we are going to write these messages as we can see in its console.

```
public class MessageReceiver : DefaultBasicConsumer
    {
        private readonly IModel _channel;

        public MessageReceiver(IModel channel)
        {
            _channel = channel;
        }

        public override void HandleBasicDeliver(string consumerTag, ulong deliveryTag, bool redelivered, string exchange, string routingKey, IBasicProperties properties, byte[] body)
        {
            Console.WriteLine($"Consuming Topic Message");
            Console.WriteLine(string.Concat("Message received from the exchange ", exchange));
            Console.WriteLine(string.Concat("Consumer tag: ", consumerTag));
            Console.WriteLine(string.Concat("Delivery tag: ", deliveryTag));
            Console.WriteLine(string.Concat("Routing tag: ", routingKey));
            Console.WriteLine(string.Concat("Message: ", Encoding.UTF8.GetString(body)));
            _channel.BasicAck(deliveryTag, false);
        }
    }
```

After completing with understanding code snippet of MessageReceiver class next we are going to calls this class in the Main method.

Code snippet of Main Method while consuming "topic.bombay.queue"

In the main method we have created connectionFactory class and passed credentials and Hostname after that we have created connection, next we have created channel and set prefetchCount to 1 such that it tells RabbitMQ not to give more than one message to a worker at a time, Next, we have created instance of MessageReceiver class and passed IModel (channel) to it, in final step we have called "**BasicConsume**" method and passed queue name to it "**topic.bombay.queue**" along with we have set autoAck to false and passed the messageReceiver instance to it.

```
using System;
using RabbitMQ.Client;

namespace RabbitMQConsumer
{
    class Program
    {
        private const string UserName = "guest";
        private const string Password = "guest";
        private const string HostName = "localhost";

        static void Main(string[] args)
        {
            ConnectionFactory connectionFactory = new ConnectionFactory
```

```
            {
                HostName = HostName,
                UserName = UserName,
                Password = Password,
            };

            var connection = connectionFactory.CreateConnection();
            var channel = connection.CreateModel();

            // accept only one unack-ed message at a time
            // uint prefetchSize, ushort prefetchCount, bool global

            channel.BasicQos(0, 1, false);

            // ==== prefetchCount
            // In order to defeat that we can set the prefetch count with the value of 1
            // This tells RabbitMQ not to give more than one message to a worker at a time.
            // Or, in other words, don't dispatch a new message to a worker until it has
            // processed and acknowledged the previous one. Instead, it will dispatch it to t
            // the next worker that is not still busy.

            MessageReceiver messageReceiver = new MessageReceiver(channel);
            channel.BasicConsume("topic.bombay.queue", false, messageReceiver);

            Console.ReadLine();
        }
    }
}
```

Now we have complete working mechanism Let's create request from "**RequestRabbitMQ**" console and consume a message from "**RabbitMQConsumer**" application.

The queue has one Request which we have published

The below snapshot contains only one message in topic.bombay.queue which we have published.

Queues

All queues (3)

Pagination

Page 1 ▼ of 1 - Filter: [   ] ☐ Regex ?

Overview			Messages			Message rates			+/-
Name	Features	State	Ready	Unacked	Total	incoming	deliver / get	ack	
request.queue	D	idle	0	0	0				
topic.bombay.queue	D	idle	1	0	1	0.00/s	0.00/s	0.00/s	
topic.delhi.queue	D	idle	0	0	0				

Consumed Message from topic.bombay.queue

```
 Consuming Topic Message
Message received from the exchange topic.exchange
Consumer tag: amq.ctag-tfp1bom4gcnoF401N-RiQA
Delivery tag: 1
Routing tag: Message.Bombay.Email
Message: Message from Topic Exchange 'Bombay'
```

After successfully consuming message from "topic.bombay.queue" next we are going to publish a message to another queue which is "topic.delhi.queue".

Published Message to topic.delhi.queue

In topicmessage class, I have just made a small change in routing key "Delhi.TicketBooking" and message which we send to publish a message to "topic.delhi.queue".

Routing pattern: - "Delhi. any text".

Examples of routing key: - "Delhi.Pizza", "Delhi.Hotels", "Delhi.Parks", "Delhi.Colleges".

Code Snippet

```csharp
public class Topicmessages
{
    private const string UserName = "guest";
    private const string Password = "guest";
    private const string HostName = "localhost";

    public void SendMessage()
    {
        //Main entry point to the RabbitMQ .NET AMQP client
        var connectionFactory = new RabbitMQ.Client.ConnectionFactory()
        {
            UserName = UserName,
            Password = Password,
            HostName = HostName
        };

        var connection = connectionFactory.CreateConnection();
        var model = connection.CreateModel();

        var properties = model.CreateBasicProperties();
        properties.Persistent = false;

        byte[] messagebuffer = Encoding.Default.GetBytes("Message from Topic Exchange 'Delhi'");

        model.BasicPublish("topic.exchange", "Delhi.TicketBooking", properties, messagebuffer);

        Console.WriteLine("Message Sent From :- topic.exchange ");
        Console.WriteLine("Routing Key :- Delhi.TicketBooking");
        Console.WriteLine("Message Sent");
    }
```

       }

After making changes let's save and run application to publish message to "topic.delhi.queue".

Published Message to "topic.delhi.queue"

```
file:///D:/RabbitMQApps/RequestRabbitMQ/RequestRabbitMQ/bin/Debug/RequestRabbitMQ.EXE
Message Sent From :- topic.exchange
Routing Key :- Delhi.TicketBooking
Message Sent
```

The queue has one Request which we have published

Queues
▼ All queues (3)

Pagination

Page 1 ▼ of 1 - Filter: [   ]   ☐ Regex ?

Overview			Messages			Message rates			+/-
Name	Features	State	Ready	Unacked	Total	incoming	deliver / get	ack	
request.queue	D	idle	0	0	0				
topic.bombay.queue	D	idle	0	0	0	0.00/s	0.00/s	0.00/s	
topic.delhi.queue	D	idle	1	0	1	0.00/s	0.00/s	0.00/s	

Code snippet of Main Method while consuming "topic.delhi.queue" from RabbitMQConsumer

In this part, I have just changed the queue name to "**topic.delhi.queue**" in RabbitMQConsumer application.

```csharp
using System;
using RabbitMQ.Client;

namespace RabbitMQConsumer
{
    class Program
    {
        private const string UserName = "guest";
        private const string Password = "guest";
        private const string HostName = "localhost";

        static void Main(string[] args)
        {
            ConnectionFactory connectionFactory = new ConnectionFactory
            {
                HostName = HostName,
                UserName = UserName,
```

```
            Password = Password,
        };
        var connection = connectionFactory.CreateConnection();
        var channel = connection.CreateModel();

        // accept only one unack-ed message at a time
        // uint prefetchSize, ushort prefetchCount, bool global

        channel.BasicQos(0, 1, false);
        // ==== prefetchCount
        // In order to defeat that we can set the prefetch count with the value of 1
        // This tells RabbitMQ not to give more than one message to a worker at a time.
        // Or, in other words, don't dispatch a new message to a worker until it has
        // processed and acknowledged the previous one. Instead, it will dispatch it to t
        // the next worker that is not still busy.

        MessageReceiver messageReceiver = new MessageReceiver(channel);
        channel.BasicConsume("topic.delhi.queue", false, messageReceiver);
        Console.ReadLine();
        }
    }
}
```

Consumed Message from topic.delhi.queue

```
Consuming Topic Message
Message received from the exchange topic.exchange
Consumer tag: amq.ctag-VLjMXHJzZqb--1q8Tt7DLw
Delivery tag: 1
Routing tag: Delhi.TicketBooking
Message: Message from Topic Exchange 'Delhi'
```

Finally, we have completed consuming Message from "**topic.delhi.queue**" queue.

Conclusion

In this article, we have learned how to use Topic Message Exchanges and how to create exchange and queue for topic exchange and how to push messages into RabbitMQ using .Net Application and RabbitMQ.Client and read messages from RabbitMQ using .Net Application and RabbitMQ.Client in step by step way.

Using RabbitMQ Fanout Message Exchanges with .Net Application

In this article, we are going to use Fanout Message Exchanges and push messages into RabbitMQ using .Net Application and RabbitMQ.Client and read messages from RabbitMQ using .Net Application and RabbitMQ.Client in step by step way.

What is a fanout exchange?

A fanout exchange routes messages to all of the queues that are bound to it.

This exchange is used when you want to publish a common message to all queue which is connected to the particular exchange and in fanout exchange **routing key** is ignored.

e.g. if a company has updated some guidelines and you want push guideline all branches that time you can use fanout exchange.

Creating RequestRabbitMQ Application

Let's Create a simple console application with Name "**RequestRabbitMQ**".

After creating application next we are going to add "**RabbitMQ.Client**" NuGet package.

Adding RabbitMQ.Client NuGet Package

In this part for creating a connection with the RabbitMQ server to create request, we need to add "RabbitMQ.Client" package from NuGet Package.

Command to install: - Install-Package RabbitMQ.Client -Version 5.1.0

```
Package Manager Console
Package source: nuget.org              Default project: RequestRabbitMQ
PM> Install-Package RabbitMQ.Client -Version 5.1.0
Attempting to gather dependency information for package 'RabbitMQ.Client.5.1.0' with respect to project
'RequestRabbitMQ', targeting '.NETFramework,Version=v4.5.2'
Attempting to resolve dependencies for package 'RabbitMQ.Client.5.1.0' with DependencyBehavior 'Lowest'
Resolving actions to install package 'RabbitMQ.Client.5.1.0'
Resolved actions to install package 'RabbitMQ.Client.5.1.0'
Adding package 'RabbitMQ.Client.5.1.0' to folder 'D:\RabbitMQApps\RequestRabbitMQ\packages'
Added package 'RabbitMQ.Client.5.1.0' to folder 'D:\RabbitMQApps\RequestRabbitMQ\packages'
Added package 'RabbitMQ.Client.5.1.0' to 'packages.config'
Successfully installed 'RabbitMQ.Client 5.1.0' to RequestRabbitMQ
PM>
```

After installing NuGet package of "**RabbitMQ.Client**" next we are going to create an exchange from web admin console.

Adding Fanout Exchange

Go to http://localhost:15672/#/exchanges , name exchange as "**fanout.exchange**" after entering name next, we select Type as "**fanout**" and click on add exchange button to create.

After adding "**fanout.exchange**" next we are going to Add 4 Queue and bind it to same exchange.

Adding queue

In this part we are going to create 4 queues with different routing key but for same "**fanout.exchange**".

Go to http://localhost:15672/#/queues

1. Mumbai
2. Hyderabad
3. Bangalore
4. Chennai

Adding the first queue with name "**Mumbai**".

▼ **Add a new queue**

Name:	Mumbai *
Durability:	Durable ▼
Auto delete: ?	No ▼
Arguments:	= String ▼
	Add Message TTL ? | Auto expire ? | Max length ? | Max length bytes ? |
	Overflow behaviour ?
	Dead letter exchange ? | Dead letter routing key ? | Maximum priority ?
	Lazy mode ? Master locator ?

[Add queue]

In a similar way, I have added rest of queues as shown in below snapshot.

Queues

▼ **All queues (4)**

Pagination

Page 1 ▼ of 1 - Filter: [   ]   ☐ Regex ?

Overview			Messages			Message rates		
Name	Features	State	Ready	Unacked	Total	incoming	deliver / get	ack
Bangalore	D	idle	0	0	0			
Chennai	D	idle	0	0	0			
Hyderabad	D	idle	0	0	0			
Mumbai	D	idle	0	0	0			

After adding all queues next we are going to bind queues with "**fanout.exchange**".

Binding the Queues (Bangalore, Chennai, Hyderabad, Mumbai) with fanout.exchange

In this part, we are binding **fanout.exchange** with all queues (Bangalore, Chennai, Hyderabad, Mumbai).

First queue we are going to bind is Bangalore.

Add binding to this queue

From exchange: `fanout.exchange` *
Routing key:
Arguments: = String

Bind

Snapshot of binding

Bindings

From	Routing key	Arguments	
(Default exchange binding)			
fanout.exchange			Unbind

⇩

This queue

An example is for Bangalore queue in a similar way we are going to do for all rest of queues which are there of fanout exchange (Chennai, Hyderabad, Mumbai).

After completing with binding next we are going to publish message

Adding a Fanoutmessages Class

we have created a "fanoutmessage" name class in this class we are going to create request and push to RabbitMQ.

First, we have declared Username, Password and HostName as constant. After that, we have created a method with name "**SendMessage**" in that message we have created a connection to RabbitMQ server using RabbitMQ.Client after creating connection next we have passed credentials along with HostName to connectionFactory. Next, we have written a simple message "**Message is of fanout Exchange type**" and got it in bytes array form, finally, we are going assign all these values to a BasicPublish method of "**RabbitMQ.Client**"

While assigning we are going to set exchange as "**fanout.exchange**" and there will not be routing key for fanout exchange.

Code Snippet

```
using System;
using RabbitMQ.Client;
using System.Text;
```

```csharp
namespace RequestRabbitMQ
{
    public class Fanoutmessages
    {
        private const string UserName = "guest";
        private const string Password = "guest";
        private const string HostName = "localhost";

        public void SendMessage()
        {
            //Main entry point to the RabbitMQ .NET AMQP client
            var connectionFactory = new RabbitMQ.Client.ConnectionFactory()
            {
                UserName = UserName,
                Password = Password,
                HostName = HostName
            };

            var connection = connectionFactory.CreateConnection();
            var model = connection.CreateModel();

            var properties = model.CreateBasicProperties();
            properties.Persistent = false;

            byte[] messagebuffer = Encoding.Default.GetBytes("Message is of fanout Exchange type");
            model.BasicPublish("fanout.exchange", "", properties, messagebuffer);
            Console.WriteLine("Message Sent From :- fanout.exchange ");
            Console.WriteLine("Routing Key :-  Routing key is Not required for fanout exchange");
            Console.WriteLine("Message Sent");
        }
    }
}
```

Main Code snippet

```csharp
using System;
namespace RequestRabbitMQ
{
    class Program
    {
        static void Main(string[] args)
        {
            Fanoutmessages fanoutmessages = new Fanoutmessages();
            fanoutmessages.SendMessage();
            Console.ReadLine();
        }
    }
}
```

After completing entire process let's save the application and run after running the application you will see a Message sent a message on a console just for notification it means we have successfully published a message to all queues of "fanout.exchange" exchange.

Published Message to all queues of "fanout.exchange"

```
file:///D:/RabbitMQApps/fanout/RequestRabbitMQ/RequestRabbitMQ/bin/Debug/RequestRabbitMQ...
Message Sent From :- fanout.exchange
Routing Key :-   Routing key is Not required for fanout exchange
Message Sent
```

Now Let's See queue status (Bangalore, Chennai, Hyderabad, Mumbai) queue

If you see Queues status you will see Ready "1" which means we have successfully published a message to all queues of fanout exchanges.

Queues

▼ All queues (4)

Pagination

Page 1 ▼ of 1 - Filter: [   ]   ☐ Regex ?

Overview			Messages			Message rates			+/-
Name	Features	State	Ready	Unacked	Total	incoming	deliver / get	ack	
Bangalore	D	idle	1	0	1	0.00/s			
Chennai	D	idle	1	0	1	0.00/s			
Hyderabad	D	idle	1	0	1	0.00/s			
Mumbai	D	idle	1	0	1	0.00/s			

After publishing a message next we are going to create .Net Console application for consuming message from the queue.

Creating RabbitMQConsumer Application

Let's create another console application for consuming messages from a queue with Name "**RabbitMQConsumer**"

```
Solution 'RabbitMQConsumer' (1 project)
  ▲ C# RabbitMQConsumer
    ▷ 🔧 Properties
    ▷ ■■ References
       🗐 App.config
    ▷ C# Program.cs
```

After creating application next we are going to add "**RabbitMQ.Client**" NuGet package.

Adding RabbitMQ.Client NuGet Package

In this part for creating a connection with the RabbitMQ server to create request, we need to add "RabbitMQ.Client" package from NuGet Package.

Command to install: - Install-Package RabbitMQ.Client -Version 5.1.0

```
Package Manager Console
Package source:  All             Default project: RabbitMQConsumer
Each package is licensed to you by its owner. NuGet is not responsible for, nor does it grant any licenses to,
third-party packages. Some packages may include dependencies which are governed by additional licenses. Follow the
package source (feed) URL to determine any dependencies.

Package Manager Console Host Version 3.4.4.1321

Type 'get-help NuGet' to see all available NuGet commands.

PM> Install-Package RabbitMQ.Client -Version 5.1.0
```

After installing RabbitMQ.Client next we are going to add a class with name "**MessageReceiver**".

Code snippet of MessageReceiver class

In this part, we have created MessageReceiver class and this class inherits DefaultBasicConsumer class which is from RabbitMQ.Client next we have to override HandleBasicDeliver method this method receives message body next, we are going to write these messages as we can see in its console.

```csharp
public class MessageReceiver : DefaultBasicConsumer
    {
        private readonly IModel _channel;

        public MessageReceiver(IModel channel)
        {
            _channel = channel;
        }

        public override void HandleBasicDeliver(string consumerTag, ulong deliveryTag, bool redelivered, string exchange, string routingKey, IBasicProperties properties, byte[] body)
        {
            Console.WriteLine($"Consuming fanout Message");
            Console.WriteLine(string.Concat("Message received from the exchange ", exchange));
            Console.WriteLine(string.Concat("Consumer tag: ", consumerTag));
            Console.WriteLine(string.Concat("Delivery tag: ", deliveryTag));
            Console.WriteLine(string.Concat("Routing tag: ", routingKey));
            Console.WriteLine(string.Concat("Message: ", Encoding.UTF8.GetString(body)));
            _channel.BasicAck(deliveryTag, false);
        }
    }
```

After completing with understanding code snippet of MessageReceiver class next we are going to calls this class in the Main method.

Code snippet of Main Method while consuming "Mumbai" queue

In the main method we have created connectionFactory class and passed credentials and Hostname after that we have created connection, next we have created channel and set prefetchCount to 1 such that it tells RabbitMQ not to give more than one message to a worker at a time, Next, we have created instance of MessageReceiver class and passed IModel (channel) to it, in final step we have called "**BasicConsume**" method and passed queue name to it "**Mumbai**" along with we have set autoAck to false and passed the messageReceiver instance to it.

```
        // uint pretetchSize, ushort pretetchCount, bool global

        channel.BasicQos(0, 1, false);

        // ==== prefetchCount
        // In order to defeat that we can set the prefetch count with the value of 1
        // This tells RabbitMQ not to give more than one message to a worker at a time.
        // Or, in other words, don't dispatch a new message to a worker until it has
        // processed and acknowledged the previous one. Instead, it will dispatch it to t
        // he next worker that is not still busy.

        MessageReceiver messageReceiver = new MessageReceiver(channel);
        channel.BasicConsume("Mumbai", false, messageReceiver);

        Console.ReadLine()
    }
}
```

(extension) string IModel.BasicConsume(string queue, bool autoAck, IBasicConsumer consumer) (+ 4 overloads)
Start a Basic content-class consumer.

```csharp
using System;
using RabbitMQ.Client;
namespace RabbitMQConsumer
{
    class Program
    {
        private const string UserName = "guest";
        private const string Password = "guest";
        private const string HostName = "localhost";

        static void Main(string[] args)
        {
            ConnectionFactory connectionFactory = new ConnectionFactory
            {
                HostName = HostName,
                UserName = UserName,
                Password = Password,
            };

            var connection = connectionFactory.CreateConnection();
            var channel = connection.CreateModel();
            // accept only one unack-ed message at a time
            // uint prefetchSize, ushort prefetchCount, bool global

            channel.BasicQos(0, 1, false);
            // ==== prefetchCount
            // In order to defeat that we can set the prefetch count with the value of 1
            // This tells RabbitMQ not to give more than one message to a worker at a time.
            // Or, in other words, don't dispatch a new message to a worker until it has
            // processed and acknowledged the previous one. Instead, it will dispatch it to t
            // the next worker that is not still busy.
            MessageReceiver messageReceiver = new MessageReceiver(channel);
            channel.BasicConsume("Mumbai", false, messageReceiver);

            Console.ReadLine();
        }
    }
}
```

Now we have complete working mechanism Let's create request from "**RequestRabbitMQ**" console and consume a message from "**RabbitMQConsumer**" application.

The queue has one Request which we have published

The below snapshot shows all queues have one message which we have published using fanout exchange.

Queues
▼ All queues (4)

Pagination

Page 1 ▼ of 1 - Filter: [   ]   ☐ Regex ?

Overview			Messages			Message rates			+/-
Name	Features	State	Ready	Unacked	Total	incoming	deliver / get	ack	
Bangalore	D	idle	1	0	1	0.00/s			
Chennai	D	idle	1	0	1	0.00/s			
Hyderabad	D	idle	1	0	1	0.00/s			
Mumbai	D	idle	1	0	1	0.00/s			

Consumed Message from Mumbai queue

This message is only consumed from Mumbai queue rest queues are unread till now.

```
Consuming fanout Message from Mumbai
Message received from the exchange fanout.exchange
Consumer tag: amq.ctag-rYWjTDJmz_GSC-3mk3D8fA
Delivery tag: 1
Routing tag:
Message: Message is of fanout Exchange type
```

The status of the queue after reading Message from Mumbai queue.

Overview			Messages			Message rates			+/-
Name	Features	State	Ready	Unacked	Total	incoming	deliver / get	ack	
Bangalore	D	idle	1	0	1	0.00/s			
Chennai	D	idle	1	0	1	0.00/s			
Hyderabad	D	idle	1	0	1	0.00/s			
Mumbai	D	idle	0	0	0	0.00/s	0.00/s	0.00/s	

In a similar way, if we read a message from Bangalore queue than just need to make a change in "**queue name**" in **RabbitMQConsumer.**

Consumed Message from Bangalore queue

We have changed just name of the queue from Mumbai to Bangalore. To read a message from Bangalore queue.

```
using System;
using RabbitMQ.Client;

namespace RabbitMQConsumer
{
    class Program
    {
        private const string UserName = "guest";
        private const string Password = "guest";
        private const string HostName = "localhost";

        static void Main(string[] args)
        {
            ConnectionFactory connectionFactory = new ConnectionFactory
            {
                HostName = HostName,
                UserName = UserName,
                Password = Password,
            };

            var connection = connectionFactory.CreateConnection();
            var channel = connection.CreateModel();

            // accept only one unack-ed message at a time
            // uint prefetchSize, ushort prefetchCount, bool global

            channel.BasicQos(0, 1, false);

            #region MyRegion
            // ==== prefetchCount
            // In order to defeat that we can set the prefetch count with the value of 1
            // This tells RabbitMQ not to give more than one message to a worker at a time.
            // Or, in other words, don't dispatch a new message to a worker until it has
            // processed and acknowledged the previous one. Instead, it will dispatch it to t
            // the next worker that is not still busy.
            #endregion

            MessageReceiver messageReceiver = new MessageReceiver(channel);
            channel.BasicConsume("Bangalore", false, messageReceiver);

            Console.ReadLine();
        }
```

```
        }
}
```

Let's save and run application to red message from Bangalore queue.

```
file:///D:/RabbitMQApps/fanout/RabbitMQConsumer/RabbitMQConsumer/bin/Debug/RabbitMQCon
Consuming fanout Message from Bangalore
Message received from the exchange fanout.exchange
Consumer tag: amq.ctag-FU117wB8EIcRBL854ROGyQ
Delivery tag: 1
Routing tag:
Message: Message is of fanout Exchange type
```

The status of the queue after reading Message from Bangalore queue.

Overview			Messages			Message rates			+/-
Name	Features	State	Ready	Unacked	Total	incoming	deliver / get	ack	
Bangalore	D	idle	0	0	0	0.00/s	0.00/s	0.00/s	
Chennai	D	idle	1	0	1	0.00/s			
Hyderabad	D	idle	1	0	1	0.00/s			
Mumbai	D	idle	0	0	0	0.00/s	0.00/s	0.00/s	

Finally, we have learned how fanout exchange works and how we can publish messages and consume messages from fanout exchange in step by step way.

Conclusion

In this article, we have learned how to use Fanout Message Exchanges and how to create exchange and queue for Fanout exchange and how to push messages into RabbitMQ using .Net Application and RabbitMQ.Client and read messages from RabbitMQ using .Net Application and RabbitMQ.Client in step by step way.

Using RabbitMQ Headers Message Exchanges with .Net Application

In this article, we are going to use Headers Message Exchanges and push messages into RabbitMQ using .Net Application and RabbitMQ.Client and read messages from RabbitMQ using .Net Application and RabbitMQ.Client in step by step way.

What is a Headers exchange?

Headers exchanges use the message header attributes for routing.

This exchange is used when you want to send a message to queue but this time it will not depend on routing key it will be sent to queue on bases of header attributes.

Creating RequestRabbitMQ Application

Let's Create a simple console application with Name "**RequestRabbitMQ**".

After creating application next we are going to add "**RabbitMQ.Client**" NuGet package.

Adding RabbitMQ.Client NuGet Package

In this part for creating a connection with the RabbitMQ server to create request, we need to add "RabbitMQ.Client" package from NuGet Package.

Command to install: - Install-Package RabbitMQ.Client -Version 5.1.0

```
Package Manager Console
Package source: nuget.org          Default project: RequestRabbitMQ
PM> Install-Package RabbitMQ.Client -Version 5.1.0
Attempting to gather dependency information for package 'RabbitMQ.Client.5.1.0' with respect to project
'RequestRabbitMQ', targeting '.NETFramework,Version=v4.5.2'
Attempting to resolve dependencies for package 'RabbitMQ.Client.5.1.0' with DependencyBehavior 'Lowest'
Resolving actions to install package 'RabbitMQ.Client.5.1.0'
Resolved actions to install package 'RabbitMQ.Client.5.1.0'
Adding package 'RabbitMQ.Client.5.1.0' to folder 'D:\RabbitMQApps\RequestRabbitMQ\packages'
Added package 'RabbitMQ.Client.5.1.0' to folder 'D:\RabbitMQApps\RequestRabbitMQ\packages'
Added package 'RabbitMQ.Client.5.1.0' to 'packages.config'
Successfully installed 'RabbitMQ.Client 5.1.0' to RequestRabbitMQ
PM>
```

After installing NuGet package of "**RabbitMQ.Client**" next we are going to create an exchange from web admin console.

Note: -

Headers exchange routes message based on header values instead of routing keys.

A special argument named x-match has 2 values {all, any} where all is the default value of a headers binding.

– x-match = all :- means that all the values must match.

– x-match = any :- means just one matching header value is sufficient.

Referenced from: - http://javasampleapproach.com/spring-framework/spring-boot/springboot-rabbitmq-headers-exchange

Adding Fanout Exchange

Go to http://localhost:15672/#/exchanges , name exchange as "**headers.exchange**" after entering name next, we select Type as "**headers**" and click on add exchange button to create.

▼ Add a new exchange

    Name: headers.exchange *
    Type: headers ▼
    Durability: Durable ▼
    Auto delete: ? No ▼
    Internal: ? No ▼
    Arguments: [   ] = [   ] String ▼
               Add **Alternate exchange** ?

Add exchange

89 | P a g e

After adding "**headers.exchange**" next we are going to Add 2 Queue and bind it to same exchange.

Adding queue

In this part, we are going to create 2 queues without different routing key but for same "**headers.exchange**".

Go to http://localhost:15672/#/queues

1. ReportPDF
2. ReportExcel

```
Add a new queue
    Name: ReportPDF
    Durability: Durable
    Auto delete: No
    Arguments:                    =                    String
        Add  Message TTL ? | Auto expire ? | Max length ? | Max length bytes ? |
             Dead letter exchange ? | Dead letter routing key ? | Maximum priority
             Lazy mode ? | Master locator ?
[Add queue]
```

In a similar way, I have added rest of queues as shown in below snapshot.

Queues

All queues (2)

Pagination

Page 1 of 1 - Filter: [ ] Regex ?

Overview			Messages			Message rates			+/-
Name	Features	State	Ready	Unacked	Total	incoming	deliver / get	ack	
ReportExcel	D	idle	0	0	0				
ReportPDF	D	idle	0	0	0				

After adding all the queues next we are going to bind queues with "**headers.exchange**".

Binding the Queues

In this part, we are binding **headers.exchange** with a "**ReportPDF**" queue and while binding we are going to set arguments such as format=pdf and x-match=all these arguments need to be passed by producer in the header such that message will be sent to the accurate queue.

Add binding to this queue

From exchange:	headers.exchange	*
Routing key:		
Arguments:	format = pdf	String ▼
	x-match = all	String ▼
	=	String ▼

[Bind]

Snapshot of binding

▼ Bindings

From	Routing key	Arguments	
(Default exchange binding)			
headers.exchange		format: pdf x-match: all	Unbind

⇩

This queue

In this part, we are binding **headers.exchange** with a "**ReportExcel**" queue and while binding we are going to set arguments such as format=pdf and x-match=all this argument needs to be passed by producer in the header such that message will be sent to the accurate queue.

Add binding to this queue

From exchange:	headers.exchange	*
Routing key:		
Arguments:	format = excel	String ▼
	x-match = all	String ▼
	=	String ▼

[Bind]

Snapshot of binding

Bindings

From	Routing key	Arguments	
(Default exchange binding)			
headers.exchange		format: excel x-match: all	Unbind

After binding all arguments to their respective queue next we are going to publish the message for that we are going to add a class.

Adding a Headersmessages Class

we have created a "Headersmessages" name class in this class we are going to create request and push to RabbitMQ.

First, we have declared Username, Password, and HostName as constant. After that, we have created a method with name "**SendMessage**" in that message we have created a connection to RabbitMQ server using RabbitMQ.Client after creating connection next we have passed credentials along with HostName to connectionFactory. Next, we have written a simple message "**Message to Headers Exchange 'format=pdf'**" and got it in bytes array form, finally, we are going assign all these values to a BasicPublish method of "**RabbitMQ.Client**"

While assigning we are going to set exchange as "**headers.exchange**" and there will not be routing key for headers exchange.

Code Snippet

```
public class Headersmessages
    {
        private const string UserName = "guest";
        private const string Password = "guest";
        private const string HostName = "localhost";

        public void SendMessage()
        {
            //Main entry point to the RabbitMQ .NET AMQP client
            var connectionFactory = new RabbitMQ.Client.ConnectionFactory()
            {
                UserName = UserName,
                Password = Password,
                HostName = HostName
            };

            var connection = connectionFactory.CreateConnection();
            var model = connection.CreateModel();

            var properties = model.CreateBasicProperties();
            properties.Persistent = false;

            Dictionary<string,object> dictionary = new Dictionary<string, object>();
            dictionary.Add("format", "pdf");
            properties.Headers = dictionary;
```

```
            byte[] messagebuffer = Encoding.Default.GetBytes("Message to Headers Exchange 
'format=pdf' ");

            model.BasicPublish("headers.exchange", "", properties, messagebuffer);

            Console.WriteLine("Message Sent From :- headers.exchange ");
            Console.WriteLine("Routing Key :- Does not need routing key");
            Console.WriteLine("Message Sent");
        }
    }
```

Main Code snippet

```
using System;
namespace RequestRabbitMQ
{
    class Program
    {
        static void Main(string[] args)
        {
            Headersmessages headersmessages = new Headersmessages();
            headersmessages.SendMessage();
            Console.ReadLine();
        }
    }
}
```

After completing entire process let's save the application and run after running the application you will see a Message sent a message on a console just for notification it means we have successfully published a message to all queues of "headers.exchange" exchange.

Published Message to Reportpdf queues of "Headers.exchange"

Now Let's See queue status

If you see Queues status of Reportpdf queue you will see Ready "1" which means, we have successfully published a message to Reportpdf queues using headers exchanges.

Queues

All queues (2)

Pagination

Page 1 ▼ of 1 - Filter: [   ] ☐ Regex ?

Overview			Messages			Message rates			+/-
Name	Features	State	Ready	Unacked	Total	incoming	deliver / get	ack	
ReportExcel	D	idle	0	0	0				
ReportPDF	D	idle	1	0	1	0.00/s			

After publishing a message next, we are going to create .Net Console application for consuming message from the queue.

Creating RabbitMQConsumer Application

Let's create another console application for consuming messages from a queue with Name "**RabbitMQConsumer**"

```
Solution 'RabbitMQConsumer' (1 project)
    RabbitMQConsumer
        Properties
        References
        App.config
        Program.cs
```

After creating application next, we are going to add "**RabbitMQ.Client**" NuGet package.

Adding RabbitMQ.Client NuGet Package

In this part for creating a connection with the RabbitMQ server to create request, we need to add "RabbitMQ.Client" package from NuGet Package.

Command to install: - Install-Package RabbitMQ.Client -Version 5.1.0

```
Package Manager Console
Package source: All          Default project: RabbitMQConsumer

Each package is licensed to you by its owner. NuGet is not responsible for, nor does it grant any licenses to,
third-party packages. Some packages may include dependencies which are governed by additional licenses. Follow the
package source (feed) URL to determine any dependencies.

Package Manager Console Host Version 3.4.4.1321

Type 'get-help NuGet' to see all available NuGet commands.

PM> Install-Package RabbitMQ.Client -Version 5.1.0
```

After installing RabbitMQ.Client next we are going to add a class with name "**MessageReceiver**".

Code snippet of MessageReceiver class

In this part, we have created MessageReceiver class and this class inherits DefaultBasicConsumer class which is from RabbitMQ.Client next we have to override HandleBasicDeliver method this method receives message body next, we are going to write these messages as we can see in its console.

```csharp
using System;
using System.Text;
using RabbitMQ.Client;

namespace RabbitMQConsumer
{
    public class MessageReceiver : DefaultBasicConsumer
    {
        private readonly IModel _channel;

        public MessageReceiver(IModel channel)
        {
            _channel = channel;
        }

        public override void HandleBasicDeliver(string consumerTag, ulong deliveryTag, bool redelivered, string exchange, string routingKey, IBasicProperties properties, byte[] body)
        {
            Console.WriteLine($"Consuming Headers Message");
            Console.WriteLine(string.Concat("Message received from the exchange ", exchange));
            Console.WriteLine(string.Concat("Consumer tag: ", consumerTag));
            Console.WriteLine(string.Concat("Delivery tag: ", deliveryTag));
            Console.WriteLine(string.Concat("Routing tag: ", routingKey));
            Console.WriteLine(string.Concat("Message: ", Encoding.UTF8.GetString(body)));
            _channel.BasicAck(deliveryTag, false);
        }
    }
}
```

After completing with understanding code snippet of MessageReceiver class next we are going to calls this class in the Main method.

Code snippet of Main Method while consuming "Mumbai" queue

In the main method we have created connectionFactory class and passed credentials and Hostname after that we have created connection, next we have created channel and set prefetchCount to 1 such that it tells RabbitMQ not to give more than one message to a worker at a time, Next, we have created instance of MessageReceiver class and passed IModel (channel) to it, in final step we have called "**BasicConsume**" method and passed queue name to it "**ReportPDF**" along with we have set autoAck to false and passed the messageReceiver instance to it.

```csharp
channel.BasicQos(0, 1, false);

// ==== prefetchCount
// In order to defeat that we can set the prefetch count with the value of 1
// This tells RabbitMQ not to give more than one message to a worker at a time.
// Or, in other words, don't dispatch a new message to a worker until it has
// processed and acknowledged the previous one. Instead, it will dispatch it to t
// he next worker that is not still busy.

MessageReceiver messageReceiver = new MessageReceiver(channel);
channel.BasicConsume("ReportPDF", false, messageReceiver);

Console.ReadLine();
```

```csharp
using System;
using RabbitMQ.Client;

namespace RabbitMQConsumer
{
    class Program
    {
        private const string UserName = "guest";
        private const string Password = "guest";
        private const string HostName = "localhost";

        static void Main(string[] args)
        {
            ConnectionFactory connectionFactory = new ConnectionFactory
            {
                HostName = HostName,
                UserName = UserName,
                Password = Password,
            };

            var connection = connectionFactory.CreateConnection();
            var channel = connection.CreateModel();

            // accept only one unack-ed message at a time
            // uint prefetchSize, ushort prefetchCount, bool global

            channel.BasicQos(0, 1, false);

            // ==== prefetchCount
            // In order to defeat that we can set the prefetch count with the value of 1
            // This tells RabbitMQ not to give more than one message to a worker at a time.
            // Or, in other words, don't dispatch a new message to a worker until it has
            // processed and acknowledged the previous one. Instead, it will dispatch it to t
            // the next worker that is not still busy.
```

```
            MessageReceiver messageReceiver = new MessageReceiver(channel);
            channel.BasicConsume("ReportPDF", false, messageReceiver);

            Console.ReadLine();
        }
    }
}
```

Now we have completed with consuming module Let's consume a message from "**ReportPDF**" queue which we have already published.

The queue has one Request which we have published

The below snapshot shows of ReportPDF queue have one message which we have published using headers exchange.

Queues
▼ All queues (2)

Pagination

Page 1 ▼ of 1 - Filter: ☐ Regex ?

Overview			Messages			Message rates			+/-
Name	Features	State	Ready	Unacked	Total	incoming	deliver / get	ack	
ReportExcel	D	idle	0	0	0				
ReportPDF	D	idle	1	0	1	0.00/s			

Consumed Message from ReportPDF queue

The snapshot while consuming message is only consumed from ReportPDF queue.

```
Consuming Headers Message
Message received from the exchange headers.exchange
Consumer tag: amq.ctag--aR6iSdJxR9Q_Y9_AC2YBA
Delivery tag: 1
Routing tag:
Message: Message to Headers Exchange 'format=pdf'
```

The status of the queue after reading Message from ReportPDF queue.

Overview			Messages			Message rates			+/-
Name	Features	State	Ready	Unacked	Total	incoming	deliver / get	ack	
ReportExcel	D	idle	0	0	0				
ReportPDF	D	idle	0	0	0	0.00/s	0.00/s	0.00/s	

We have completed consuming messages from ReportPDF queue.

Conclusion

In this article, we have learned how to use headers Message Exchanges and how to create exchange and queue for headers exchange and how to push messages into RabbitMQ using .Net Application and RabbitMQ.Client and read messages from RabbitMQ using .Net Application and RabbitMQ.Client in step by step way.

Author

Saineshwar Bageri (sai)

Microsoft MVP | C# Corner MVP | FULL STACK .NET Developer

Find me on: -

https://mvp.microsoft.com/en-us/PublicProfile/5003160?fullName=Saineshwar%20%20Bageri

https://www.c-sharpcorner.com/members/saineshwar-bageri

https://www.codeproject.com/Members/saineshwarbageri

https://stackoverflow.com/users/1234855/saineshwar?tab=profile

Useful Links

- Source Code Download Link: -   https://github.com/saineshwar/RabbitMQ
- Read Articles: -   https://www.tutlane.com/tutorial/rabbitmq

Reference

- http://rabbitmq.com
- https://www.cloudamqp.com

NuGet's

- RabbitMQ.Client

Now that you've read the book...

TELL US WHAT YOU THINK!

WAS IT USEFUL?
DID IT TEACH YOU WHAT YOU WANTED TO LEARN?
WAS THERE ROOM FOR IMPROVEMENT?

Let us know at-
saineshwarbageri@outlook.com

Manufactured by Amazon.ca
Bolton, ON